MW00778293

DISCARD

American Plants for American Gardens

American Plants for American Gardens

EDITH A. ROBERTS

and

ELSA REHMANN

Foreword by Darrel G. Morrison

The University of Georgia Press
Athens & London

Published in 1996 by the University of Georgia Press
Athens, Georgia 30602
© 1929 by the Macmillan Company
Foreword to this edition © 1996 by the
University of Georgia Press
All rights reserved

Printed in the United States of America

Library of Congress Cataloging in Publication Data

Roberts, Edith Adelaide, b. 1881.
American plants for American gardens / Edith A. Roberts and
Elsa Rehmann ; foreword by Darrel G. Morrison.
p   cm.
Originally published: New York : The Macmillan Company, 1929.
Includes index.
ISBN 0-8203-1851-5 (alk. paper)
1. Native plant gardening—East (U.S.) 2. Native plants for
cultivation—East (U.S.) 3. Landscape gardening—East (U.S.)
4. Landscape plants—East (U.S.) I. Rehmann, Elsa. II. Title.
SB439.24.E3R635 1996
635.9'5174—dc20   96-11362

British Library Cataloging in Publication Data available

ACKNOWLEDGMENTS

In 1924, the Conservation Committee of The Garden Club of America published with the Bulletin a booklet by Edith A. Roberts and Margaret F. Shaw on The Ecology of the Plants Native to Dutchess County, New York. This booklet with its lists of plants arranged according to ecological associations suggested the idea for a series of articles which appeared in *House Beautiful* under the title of Plant Ecology and are now presented in this book.

CONTENTS

In accordance with provisions of the International Code of Botanical Nomenclature, many of the scientific names of plant species included in the community lists in *American Plants for American Gardens* have been changed since the 1929 publication date. Grateful acknowledgment is made to Dr. Haynes Currie for contributing his expertise in plant taxonomy to update the plant lists to the current nomenclature. The 1929 names have been retained in the plant lists within the text; the old and the new nomenclature for plants whose names have been changed are included in an appendix at the end of the book under the appropriate plant-community heading.

FOREWORD

DARREL G. MORRISON

I was first introduced to *American Plants for American Gardens* in 1963, while working as a fledgling landscape architect in the Washington, D.C., area. At that time, the book had been published more than three decades earlier, in 1929, and was authored by two faculty members at Vassar College: Dr. Edith Roberts, professor of botany, and Elsa Rehmann, landscape architect, writer, and lecturer on landscape gardening. Now, at a time when we often lament the loss of a sense of place, and as "sustainability" becomes an increasingly popular catchword in landscape design and management, this volume has a message that is as valid today as it was the day it was published: the naturally evolved associations of native plants within a particular region can provide both information and inspiration for the design of gardens and landscapes that are ecologically sound and aesthetically satisfying. Furthermore, by utilizing patterns and processes that are intrinsic to naturally evolved landscapes, we can create designed and managed landscapes that are clearly "of the place" and that approach the ideal of sustainability. By conscientiously following this model, we can also protect biological diversity in the human-dominated landscape. The fact that these ideas are extremely relevant in today's world testifies to the initial viability of Roberts and Rehmann's compact volume, as well as to its long-term logic, its own sustainability over the decades.

Sadly, much of that logic failed to flow into the mainstream of landscape design and management practices during several of the intervening decades between the book's first publication and the present. It has been only since the 1970s, following the first Earth Day in this country, that many of the ideas advanced in *American Plants for American Gardens* have resurfaced in the literature of landscape architecture. Today, native landscape proponents in this country are viewed with a certain skepticism and even suspicion in some quarters.

The seeming disappearance of Roberts and Rehmann's ideas during the mid-twentieth century, and their more recent resurgence, will be treated later in this foreword. First, however, their work will be placed in the context of the flow of events in the authors' two complementary but different disciplines: plant ecology (Roberts) and landscape architecture (Rehmann). It should be noted that *American Plants for American Gardens* is a slightly revised compilation of twelve articles first published in *House Beautiful* magazine between June 1927 and May 1928 under the general heading "Plant Ecology." The authors observe in the first article of the series and in chapter one of the book that plant ecology is "a comparatively new study of plants in relation to their environment."

PLANT ECOLOGY UP TO THE 1920S

Coined in 1866 by Ernst Haeckel, the term "oecologie" derives from the Greek "oikos," which originally referred to the family household or home and its daily operation and management. But it was not until 1895 when Danish professor Eugenius Warming published his treatise, *Plantesamfund*, that a concept of plant communities was explicitly advanced (Worster 1985). The translation of Warming's work into English was entitled *The Oecology of Plants: An Introduction to the Study of Plant Communities*. In this work, Warming recognizes plant communities as dynamic changing systems, a theme that was further developed independently by American ecologists Frederic Clements of the University of Nebraska and Henry C. Cowles of the University of Chicago. Cowles's paper, "The Ecological Relations of the Vegetation on the Sand Dunes of Lake Michigan" (1899), became a classic case study of the dynamics within a specific ecosystem. Clements's treatise, "Plant Succession" (1916), while subject to later ecologists' questioning and to the advancement of alternative theories and refinements, was a seminal work in the literature of plant community development.

The publication of Cowles's study of the lake dunes plant communities placed him at the forefront of the young field of plant ecology at the turn of the century, both in this country and abroad, according to Worster. Subsequent to that publication, Cowles immersed himself in teaching at his alma mater, the University of Chicago, from 1902 until 1934. He became editor of the journal *Botanical Gazette* in 1926 but published little himself during the period that he was teaching.

Cowles's place in the history of ecological thought is secure, nonetheless, since he taught and provided intellectual inspiration to a whole series of students who themselves became leaders in the young field of plant ecology (Worster 1985). Significant to our purposes here, one of the many students who benefitted from Cowles's inspiring teaching was Edith Roberts, coauthor of *American Plants for American Gardens*. She received her Ph.D. from the University of Chicago in 1915, the same year Dr. Cowles became a full professor there. Subsequently, Roberts became a faculty member in botany at Vassar College, where she taught from 1919 until 1950. Clearly, when she undertook the "Plant Ecology" series for *House Beautiful* with Elsa Rehmann, she was writing from a very solid background in "the comparatively new study of plants in relation to their environment."

Foreword

THE PRAIRIE STYLE
AND OTHER NATIVE LANDSCAPE TRENDS

While a student of Cowles's at the University of Chicago, Edith Roberts could hardly have missed exposure to an important strand in the development of landscape architecture that was particularly strong in the Midwest, most notably in Chicago. This came to be known as the prairie style of landscape design. It developed in parallel with the better known prairie school of architecture whose most famous practitioners were Louis Sullivan and Frank Lloyd Wright. Just as the architecture of the prairie school drew on the horizontality of the midwestern prairie as a central theme, the prairie style of landscape design repeated the horizontal lines of the prairie in landforms, stratified stonework, and the branching habits of plants. Furthermore, practitioners of the prairie style placed a high priority on conserving the native flora and using it in designed settings (Grese 1992).

Perhaps the most well-known prairie style practitioner was Danish-born landscape architect Jens Jensen, who worked in Chicago from 1884 (soon after arriving in this country in his early twenties) until 1935, when he moved to Door County, Wisconsin, to establish the Clearing, a "school of the soil." During his career, he worked for both the Chicago park system and in an extensive private practice that included limited collaboration with both Louis Sullivan and Frank Lloyd Wright. As early as 1888, Jensen established the American Garden in a corner of Chicago's Union Park while an employee of the West Parks. Increasingly throughout his long and productive career, Jensen espoused the use of native plants in designed landscapes and the study of naturally evolving landscapes as sources of inspiration for design.

One of Jensen's most frequent companions in exploring native midwestern landscapes was Dr. Henry C. Cowles of the

University of Chicago, Edith Roberts's major professor. Cowles was a member of the Prairie Club, a group formed by Jensen and others in 1908 that organized field trips to natural areas in the Chicago region and throughout Illinois, Indiana, and Wisconsin (Grese 1992). Subsequently, Cowles became a member of Jensen's influential conservation organization, Friends of Our Native Landscape, when it was formed in 1913.

From 1911 to 1915, while she was working on her M.S. and Ph.D. degrees under Dr. Cowles, Roberts certainly became familiar with the philosophy and practice of the prairie style of landscape design, particularly the style of Cowles's good friend Jens Jensen. She may well have gone on outings with Friends of Our Native Landscape before completing her degree program in 1915. Undoubtedly, she viewed Jensen's park design work in Chicago. One of the many parks in the Chicago Park System that he designed and one that clearly demonstrated many of his design principles was Humboldt Park, which he worked on intermittently from 1907 until 1917. It was in this park that Jensen first developed a "prairie river" as a design feature inspired by naturally occurring rivers in the region (Grese 1992).

Jensen was not alone in the field of landscape architecture in his passion for using natural models as inspiration for designed landscapes. Among other early proponents of this approach was O. C. Simonds. Simonds studied architecture and civil engineering at the University of Michigan, and in 1881 he became superintendent of Chicago's Graceland Cemetery. In his work there, as well as in a broad-ranging design practice including cemeteries, campuses, parks, and residences, Simonds used local landforms and native vegetation to express regional character (Grese 1992).

Another important link in the chain of nature-inspired landscape design and conservation proponents in the Midwest was Wilhelm Miller, landscape architect and writer. After earning degrees from the University of Michigan in 1892 and Cornell University in 1899, Miller joined the editorial staff of *Country Life in America* (1901–1912) and edited *Garden Magazine* from 1905 to 1912. In 1912, he joined the faculty of landscape horticulture at the University of Illinois, and in 1914 he was appointed head of the division of landscape extension there. In that capacity, Miller published *The Prairie Spirit in Landscape Gardening* (1915) as an extension publication featuring the work of Jensen, Simonds, and architect/landscape architect Walter Burley Griffin. This publication played an important role in establishing the prairie style of landscape design as an identifiable and influential movement within landscape architecture.

Meanwhile in the East, another strong proponent of native-inspired landscape design was Frank Waugh, who established the department of landscape gardening at Massachusetts Agricultural College (now the University of Massachusetts) in Amherst after his appointment as a faculty member in 1902. Waugh strongly advocated field observation of natural landscapes as a basis for landscape design in his teaching and in his prolific writings, including many articles in the periodicals *Landscape Architecture* and *American Landscape Architect*. His book advocating this approach, *The Natural Style of Landscape Gardening*, was published in 1917.

Waugh was born and educated in the Midwest and was strongly influenced by the ideas of Jensen and Miller, but he developed his own emphasis on understanding, interpreting, and clarifying "the spirit of the place" (McLelland 1993). Furthermore, in many cases Waugh was a proponent of "intelligently letting alone a natural landscape." He closely followed developments in the young discipline of plant ecology and drew on them in his own teaching and writing. In *The Natural Style of Landscape Gardening*, Waugh referred directly to the emerging concepts of plant communities when he wrote: "Practically every [plant species] is associated habitually with certain other species. Thus they form set clubs or societies. And these friendly associations, based upon similarity of tastes and complementary habits of growth, should not be broken up. If we as landscape gardeners desire to preserve the whole aspect of nature, with all its forms intact, we will keep all plants in their proper social groupings" (McLelland 1993).

On the West Coast during the early twentieth century, Gustav Stickley similarly advocated cooperation with nature and harmony between the building and the site in his journal the *Craftsman*. Features in that publication, such as the 1909 article "The Natural Garden: Some Things That Can Be Done When Nature is Followed Instead of Thwarted," helped to advance the concept of native, natural gardens in California (McLelland 1993).

In 1927, the year in which Roberts and Rehmann published their first articles in the plant ecology series in *House Beautiful*, the venerable Olmsted Brothers' landscape architectural firm from Brookline, Massachusetts, designed a "wild garden and native plant preserve" for the Ahwahnee Hotel in Yosemite National Park's Yosemite Valley. The site was particularly amenable to such a design, with a variety of microhabitats represented: shaded woodlands, dry granitic rock outcroppings, and wet meadows. The success of this project and its popularity with the public provided a stimulus for the National Park Service to expand the concept to other parts of Yosemite and to other western parks (McLelland 1993). Subsequently, in the 1930s, nurseries for the propagation and growth of native plants were established in national parks ranging from Acadia National Park in Maine to Sequoia National Park in California, as well as in many state parks.

In 1930, the National Park Service adopted a policy of "landscape naturalization" under the leadership of Harold C. Bryant, assistant director for education. Under this policy, exotic plants were banned in any new landscape development and removal of any already-present exotics was encouraged. In his "Set of Ideals" outlining these policies, Bryant notes that "the introduction of exotic species endangers the native forms through competition and destroys the normal flora and fauna and . . . it is the duty of the National Park Service to protect nature unchanged for the benefit of this and future generations" (McLelland 1993). We know today how well-founded Bryant's concern about exotic plants' invasiveness was, since this problem is one of the major threats to the integrity of most "natural" areas.

From this cross section of native landscape-oriented activities during the first three decades of the twentieth century, it is apparent that there was, at the time Roberts and Rehmann produced *American Plants for American Gardens*, broad professional interest in the use of native plants in ecologically based groupings, as well as in the study of natural landscapes as a basis for design, and there was even an early awareness of the potential invasiveness of introduced exotics.

THE DECLINE OF ECOLOGICALLY BASED DESIGN

Sometime between 1929 and 1996, the seemingly strong current that linked principles of plant ecology with the practice of landscape design was subsumed within a landscape architectural mainstream that largely ignored those principles. How else do we explain the vast majority of contemporary American-designed landscapes in the last half of the twentieth century? The landscapes of residential subdivisions, corporate campuses, and even public parks, with a few notable exceptions, are based on irrigation- and chemical-dependent expanses of turf grass, beds of mulch or single-species ground covers, and a mix of broadly adapted trees and shrubs dominated by a few widely used species, some of which may be native. Even when native species are present, though, they rarely are assembled to represent plant communities of the region. Hence, the designed and managed landscapes of one region increasingly tend to look like those of every other region. At the same time, they resemble the naturally evolving landscapes of their own region less and less.

So what were the factors that led to the demise of the movement toward a natural style of landscape gardening that seemed to be so strong in the 1920s? To trace the complex set of influences that seem to have conspired against this approach could easily be the subject of an entire book itself. This discussion will suggest some of the major factors and trends that became obstacles to the widespread adoption of principles espoused by Jens Jensen, Wilhelm Miller, Frank Waugh, Edith Roberts, and Elsa Rehmann, among others.

1. *The End of the Estate Era.* With the stock market crash of 1929, the year that *American Plants for American Gardens* was first published, and with the cataclysmic economic depression that ensued, the era of designing gardens for large private estates essentially ended. Much of the work that provided practitioners like Jensen the opportunity to design significant native gardens had been private estate design for wealthy industrialists. Roberts and Rehmann's book is oriented toward the design of private estate landscapes as well, although not necessarily large ones.

But even as the estate era in landscape design was ending, public work increased, particularly in response to the formation of the Civilian Conservation Corps (CCC), which carried out major landscape and construction projects in national and state parks between 1933 and 1942. This decade was in a sense a golden era in public landscape work, and the park work of the CCC crews throughout the period generally held steadfastly to the tenets of ecologically based design, construction, and management that had been developed within the National Park Service during the 1920s and early 1930s. After 1942 however, with the termination of the CCC, with changes in administrative structure within the National Park Service, and with increasing pressures for greater efficiency and expediency, those earlier principles were often sacrificed (McLelland 1993).

2. *The Modern Movement in Landscape Architecture.* A powerful force in the development of American landscape architecture was the modernist movement of the 1930s. Three of the acknowledged leaders of this movement were Garrett Eckbo, Daniel Kiley, and James Rose, all of whom were students at Harvard during this period and who in their way were rebelling against both beaux arts formalism and the naturalism practiced by Frederick Law Olmsted. With references to both modern painting and modern architecture (e.g., the work of Mies van der Rohe), the modernists were centrally concerned with spatial structure and (to some degree) with shapes, such as those adapted from cubist paintings: "the zigzag and the piano curve, for example, executed in flowers, paving, or even terrace walls" (Treib 1993). Plants contributed to the spatial structure of the modernists, but primarily as structural elements. Furthermore, modernist theory suggested that plants, in order to achieve their fullest potential as sculptural entities, should be planted as individual specimens. With emphasis on plants as architectural and/or sculptural elements, species selection was based more on plant form (e.g., columnar, horizontal, pendulous, round or oval, irregular and picturesque) than on whether they were native to the region

in which they were planted (Trieb 1993). And in their opposi-
tion to mass planting and Olmstedian naturalism, the modernists' planting design almost by definition eliminated the assemblage
of plants in community-like groupings.

3. *Post–World War II Suburbanization.* During World War II,
any type of garden—other than the "victory" vegetable garden—
took a back seat to the war effort. In the years following the war,
a massive wave of construction began on many fronts. Subdivisions of small houses on small lots proliferated at the edges of
cities and towns. Neighborhood shopping centers followed, and
the Interstate Highway System was initiated soon after. The push
toward efficiency and expediency that was felt in the landscape
practices of the National Park Service after 1942 was magnified
many times over in this wave of construction, and the preservation and use of native plant communities took a very low priority.

The suburbanization process that began in the years immediately following the Second World War has continued ever since,
with only a few slow periods during economic slumps. By the
1970s and 1980s, subdivision houses had become typically larger
than their 1950s precursors, and shopping centers had become
large and enclosed regional-market malls. Furthermore, new
commercial/residential/office complexes popped up along perimeter highways (and then along *outer* perimeter highways) as a new
phenomenon, called "Edge Cities" by Garreau, evolved (Garreau
1991). Relative to the natural environment in these cities, Garreau
wryly notes that there are two laws governing the naming of
developments: "You name a place for what is no longer there as
a result of your actions," and "All subdivisions are named after
whatever species are first driven out by the construction. E.g.:
Quail Trail Estates" (Garreau 1991).

4. *The Landscape Industry.* With the suburbanization of America, one of the major growth industries during the last half-century has been what might collectively be called the landscape industry: plant nurseries, irrigation companies, lawn and garden equipment manufacturers, chemical fertilizer and pesticide producers, and lawn care companies. As some indication of the magnitude of these enterprises, lawns now cover twenty-five million acres in this country, giving rise to a twenty-five billion-dollar-a-year turfgrass industry (Bormann, et al. 1993). The various components of the landscape industry have been quite effective at marketing not only their products but also an aesthetic standard for "developed" landscapes as they replace the previously existing forests, fields, prairies, and wetlands that once surrounded our cities and towns.

5. *Landscape Architectural Education.* In their own way, schools of landscape architecture have been cooperators if not actual facilitators of a standardized landscape aesthetic in this country as well. For decades, traditional plant materials courses have focused on a nearly standard list of trees and shrubs with some regional variation due to climatic differences. For the most part, the plants that are featured in these courses are widely adapted species that are mass-produced by large-scale nurseries, with a preponderance of introduced species and cultivars. Courses that feature herbaceous plants are only occasionally available to landscape architecture students. While ecological concepts may be taught in the basic curriculum, very few courses on local plant communities are available, and even fewer courses that provide field observation and interpretation of native plant communities are offered. Planting design in most programs has been reduced to a one-term course. This is in sharp contrast with the emphasis it received at Lowthorpe School when Elsa Rehmann

attended (MacKechnie 1995). Lowthorpe School was founded in 1901 in Groton, Massachusetts, and devoted itself "exclusively to training women for the profession of landscape architecture" (Merrell 1926). In that program, great attention was given to plant science, including hands-on experience with propagation and culture of a wide variety of species; and planting design was a central component of the studio course sequence.

REEMERGENCE OF ECOLOGICAL DESIGN

During the last thirty years, new interest in ecologically based landscape design has reemerged as a topic in the literature, and occasionally in the practice, of landscape architecture. Ian McHarg's landmark book, *Design with Nature* (1966), stimulated a new awareness of the importance of considering ecological and environmental factors in large-scale land planning. In *Design with Nature*, McHarg does not purport to delve into the design of individual sites or gardens with nature foremost in mind, but in some cases he does lead to a framework of more environmentally sensitive land-development policies and practices within which existing native plant communities are preserved.

Other influences have contributed to a renewed interest in bringing concepts of ecology to the design of individual sites and gardens. The first Earth Day, April 22, 1970, played a role by raising public awareness of broad issues such as the need for protecting plant and animal species from extinction as well as specific perils such as those associated with pesticide use in homes and gardens. Current and impending water shortages, especially in the West and Southwest, have encouraged people to consider "xeriscaping" and other water-conserving landscape practices, including the use of drought-adapted native plants in the design of their gardens.

Foreword

Popular books, such as Sara Stein's *Noah's Garden: Restoring the Ecology of Our Own Back Yards* (1993), have made people more aware of the possibility of having a richer home environment for themselves while providing a habitat for birds, butterflies, and small mammals at the same time. Similarly, *Redesigning the American Lawn* by F. Herbert Bormann, Diana Balmori, and Gordon T. Geballe (1993), describes some of the problems associated with our twenty-five million acres of turfgrass in this country and advances strategies for replacing some of those acres of lawn with biotically richer alternatives.

On April 26, 1994, President Clinton released a Presidential Memorandum to all federal agencies in which he called for "Environmentally and Economically Beneficial Landscape Practices" to be employed on all new federal or federally funded project sites. Central to his request are the provisions for using regionally appropriate native plants, protecting natural habitats on construction sites, minimizing the use of chemicals in landscape management, and practicing water conservation. The guidelines that have been developed for the implementation of these provisions, in many respects, would be met by following the design approach proposed in Roberts and Rehmann's *American Plants for American Gardens*.

THE SIGNIFICANCE OF
American Plants for American Gardens TODAY

Today's world differs from the world of 1929 in many areas, including social, political, economic, and environmental concerns. Environmentally, we are beginning to recognize the magnitude of global changes that have been wrought by the actions of humans and the potential for even greater changes in the future. Books such as Bill McKibben's *The End of Nature* (1990), Albert

Gore's *Earth in the Balance* (1992), and E. O. Wilson's *The Diversity of Life* (1992) remind us of these changes as well as the fact that it is in our own long-term best interest to modify our resource-consumption habits and to recognize our reliance on other forms of life for our own survival.

So what does a little book on native American plants for American gardens, written by two Vassar faculty members in the 1920s, have to offer that can begin to make a dent in the environmental problems facing us at the end of the twentieth century? For one, the studies of the open field, the juniper hillside, the oak woods, the stream-side, and other plant communities included in *American Plants for American Gardens* provide models that enable us to see more clearly the beauty of these and other once-common native associations wherever we might live. They provide a way of looking at our natural environment and suggest that an attitude of humility be adopted as we manipulate that environment.

For landscape architects working in northeastern states, the plant lists and accompanying texts provide valuable information for the design and management of a wide range of project types, which include not only residential properties but also school grounds, corporate office sites, roadways, and parks. Sadly today, many of the native communities have been invaded by introduced species such as purple loosestrife (*Lythrum salicaria*), buckthorn (*Rhamnus cathartica*), Norway maple (*Acer platanoides*), and imported honeysuckles (*Lonicera* spp.), to name a few, and we need to recognize that these have, in many instances, diminished the natural diversity of the sites that they have invaded. (Ironically, if landscape architects and nurserymen had wholeheartedly embraced the philosophy advanced in *American Plants for American Gardens* throughout the last sixty-five years, this problem would most likely be much less serious than it is.) Restoring the visual and botanical characteristics of the native communities to thei earlier condition will require eradication of these pests as we as constant vigilance and hands-on management to hold ther at bay. But the rewards of restoring the qualities of natural com munities are great, not the least of which is to provide a hom for native species that otherwise are disappearing from the worlc

In an article written for *Landscape Architecture* magazine in 193: Elsa Rehmann illustrated a vision for the application of prin ciples found in *American Plants for American Gardens*, that is, th application of ecological understanding in a wide variety of situ ations far broader than individual gardens and private estate: In that article, Rehmann provides the following observations: "Fo a book of its kind and size, the authors had to content them selves with a rather set plan and with suggestions which wer limited to the private estate. But, with a little ingenuity on th part of the reader, the book can be adapted for wider use. It can for instance, be used as a field book since it is really a primer to more comprehensive understanding of native plants as well a to a keener appreciation of the relationship inherent between nativ vegetation and the landscape. It is this inherent relationship tha many a landscape architect seems to forget in his eagerness t organize land and landscape for human use and to show his cre ative ability as an artist" (Rehmann 1933).

In the same article, she notes the importance of close, first hand observation as a method of understanding landscape, a activity that is just as useful today as it was in 1929:

> Intensive observation of the landscape, observation eco-
> logically attuned, is of course the best schooling. Scenes of
> great beauty are to be found everywhere,—laurel-filled oak
> woods; hemlock woods where yews spread their needled
> branches under the trees; hillsides where cedars stand in

monumental arrangements or group themselves in a seemingly more spontaneous manner with ground junipers, wild
roses, and sometimes bayberries, sweetferns, and huckleberries; tumbling brooks between fern-encrusted ledges; streams
flowing slowly through luxuriant water-loving vegetation.
Here are some of the scenes that are ready with many a
suggestion for garden use. To be naturalistic, in the truest
sense, the plants have to be assembled in compositions that
are true reproductions or sympathetic interpretations of the
landscape scene. (Rehmann 1933)

This vivid description depicting the joys of ecologically based
landscape design reveals the keen eye of a passionate observer.
American Plants for American Gardens stems from this passion.
Hopefully with the distribution of this new edition, respect and
admiration for indigenous plants and naturalistic settings will
be heightened, along with efforts to restore them to designed and
managed landscapes as well as to preserve them in areas where
they already exist.

Works Cited

Bormann, F. Herbert, Diana Balmori, and Gordon T. Geballe. *Redesigning the American Lawn: A Search for Environmental Harmony*. New Haven: Yale University Press, 1993.

Clements, Frederic E. *Plant Succession: An Analysis of the Development of Vegetation*. Washington, D.C.: National Academy of Sciences, 1916.

Cowles, Henry C. "The Ecological Relations of the Vegetation on the Sand Dunes of Lake Michigan." *Botanical Gazette* 27 (1899): 97–117, 167–202, 281–308, 361–91.

Garreau, Joel. *Edge Cities*. Garden City, N.Y.: Doubleday, 1991.

Gore, Albert. *Earth in the Balance*. New York: Houghton Mifflin, 1992.

Grese, Robert E. *Jens Jensen: Maker of Natural Parks and Gardens*. Baltimore:

Foreword

Johns Hopkins University Press, 1992.

McHarg, Ian. *Design with Nature*. Garden City, N.Y.: Doubleday, 1966.

MacKechnie, Nancy, Curator of Rare Books and Manuscripts, Vassar College Libraries. Telephone interview by author, July 13, 1995.

McKibben, Bill. *The End of Nature*. New York: Random House, 1990.

McLelland, Linda Flint. *See* U.S. Department of the Interior.

Merrell, Mrs. Cyrus Winslow. "Lowthorpe." *Landscape Architecture* 15 (1925): 4, 262–64.

Miller, Wilhelm, *The Prairie Spirit in Landscape Gardening*. Circular no. 184. Agricultural Experiment Station, Department of Horticulture, University of Illinois, Urbana, 1915.

Rehmann, Elsa. "An Ecological Approach." *Landscape Architecture* 23 (1933): 4, 239–46.

Stein, Sara. *Noah's Garden: Restoring the Ecology of Our Own Back Yards*. New York: Houghton Mifflin, 1993.

Treib, Marc. "Axioms for a Modern Landscape Architecture." In *Modern Landscape Architecture: A Critical Review*, edited by Marc Treib. Cambridge: MIT Press, 1993.

U.S. Department of the Interior. National Park Service. *Presenting Nature: The Historic Landscape Design of the National Park Service 1916 to 1942*, by Linda Flint McLelland. Washington, D.C., 1993.

Waugh, Frank A. *The Natural Style in Landscape Gardening*. Boston: Richard G. Badger, 1917.

Wilson, Edward O. *The Diversity of Life*. Cambridge: Harvard University Press, 1992.

Worster, Donald. *Nature's Economy: A History of Ecological Ideas*. Cambridge: Cambridge University Press, 1985.

American Plants for
American Gardens

CHAPTER I

THE beauty and variety of plants native to America have ever been recognized and have made a deep impression upon the plant lover. Plant ecology, a comparatively new study of plants in relation to their environment, contributes toward a keener understanding of this natural vegetation and its use in garden making. It draws attention to the native plants as they appear in the landscape and suggests their inherent appropriateness to grounds and gardens.

It is almost unbelievable that the native plants should ever have been overlooked. Yet little use of them was made in the seventeenth century gardens where plants from the Old World flourished. And even during much of the eighteenth and nineteenth centuries they were neglected.

Many outstanding native plants have, however, been in use now for a long time. They have been planted as specimens, in miscellaneous groups, in formal arrangements and in naturalistic compositions. Some of these have, indeed, been collected into what are called native gardens. And the demand for them is ever increasing. They fit into the informal, intimate, seemingly unstudied effects that are sought for in many grounds and gardens to-day where flowers are luxuriantly intermingled, boundaries are freely planted, trees are irregularly grouped and lawns are sometimes left unclipped. More than this, the very landscape of which they are so vital a part is beginning to be retained and recreated as a setting for the house. Great trees are kept as a background for it. And all around, there are rocky slopes, shady woods, sunny meadows, ponds and stream-sides, and sometimes even bogs, that make natural gardens. When these scenes have to be recreated, the choice of the plants may be focused upon those that really belong to the particular scene and the compositions made of them may be true reproductions or sympathetic interpretations of the landscape. In such preservation and in such recreation, then, plant ecology can be of invaluable assistance and suggestion.

In plant ecology, observations are made as to what plants grow together and how they compose the groups known as plant associations. Observations are also made of what the plants in each association have in common as to soil, light, moisture and temperature, all of which are the factors which make up what is called the plants' environment. These observations draw attention to the fact that every slight variation in any one of these factors changes the members of each association and brings about the infinite variety that exists in the natural grouping of plants.

Introduction

The natural distribution of plants over the world is controlled in part by temperature, moisture and light; that is, by climatic conditions. This is made evident by the distinctive regional segregation of plants in the United States; by the palms of semitropical Florida; by the grasslands of the Mississippi Valley; by the gray-green vegetation of the Southwest; by the cacti, yuccas and agaves of the desert; by the coniferous forests of the West Coast; and by the dominantly deciduous growth of the Northeastern States.

It is the vegetation of the Northeastern States, from the Atlantic west over the Alleghenies and south to Georgia, that is discussed in this book to show the use of ecology in selecting American plant material for American grounds and gardens.

All vegetation is assembled into distinct groupings through its inherent adaptation to the environment in which it grows. For convenience, each of these groupings, or plant associations, is given the name of some tree which is prominent in the group, or is described by the situation in which it is found. Many different associations may be seen in any trip along a country road in this region, as the road winds up hill and down dale, from mountain top to river valley; as it passes rocky wooded uplands, sunny fields, cool ravines and low-lying meadows with bogs, ponds and streams. The associations will be recognized when attention is given to the various plant groups that are gathered together, and to the topography of the landscape as a whole.

Asters and the golden-rods, prominent though they

[3]

are, are only two among the many plants that grow together in the open fields; and the juniper, for all its importance, is one of a small number that adapts itself to exposed slopes. Gray birches belong in a group composed of delicate ground covers and but this one tree. The pines are the only trees of their group. The dogwoods, that have such an outstanding decorative quality, grow in upland areas of oak woods along with a rich variety of trees and shrubs, such as azaleas, laurels, huckleberries, maple-leaved viburnums, witch-hazels, sassafras, hickories and tulip trees. Beeches, maples and hemlocks are the prominent trees in other forests on the hillsides, and the hemlocks belong with ferns and other plants in cool, shady ravines. Other groups of plants are found in low-lying places. The marsh marigold is but one of many herbaceous plants that grow with trees and shrubs along streams. The water lily is surrounded by plants that require quiet, aquatic conditions. The pitcher plant belongs to an unusual vegetation that can endure the adverse conditions of the bog; and the bayberry is found with the plants that thrive on windy seashores.

Each of these groups is given a chapter in this book. The most important plants are mentioned, the fundamentals that underly each association are indicated, the natural compositions that they make are suggested, and the way they can be used about the house and in relation to it are outlined. In order to emphasize the outstanding characteristics, the descriptions are focused upon the period in the life of each association when its dominant members reach maturity.

Nature is, however, always in transition. One plant group is no sooner established than its very development changes the light, the temperature and moisture conditions to such a degree that a new group comes in and succeeds the first. The definiteness of these transitions is shown by the way in which the junipers, the gray birches, the pines, the oaks and the maple, beech or hemlocks follow one another in succession. On the uplands the open fields are filled with sun-loving herbs and shrubs. They make a congenial place for the germination of juniper seeds. The shade and protection of the junipers encourages the development of the seed of the birches. Birch copses in their turn are nurseries for the pines. The pine green, too dense for its own seed, provides the right conditions for the oaks. In their maturity the oaks make an excellent environment for the development of the maple, beech and hemlocks. All three of these spring up within their own shade, but where the shade becomes deepest and where it is coolest the hemlocks dominate.

The abandoned farm illustrates what happens to an environment, within a generation or two, when nature is left to run its own course. The once cultivated fields are soon covered with shrubs and herbs, then junipers, which are followed quickly by gray birches, and then pines. The wood lot left to itself, changes from pine to oak. The rarer old, old woods that have never been touched by woodcutters have gone through these successions and remain as rich forest lands of beech, maple or hemlock.

Nature is ever tending toward the most luxuriant form of vegetation which environmental factors permit, and in the region described it is reached in the beech-maple-hemlock forest. Such factors as the exposure upon the seashore, the lack of water on the dry hillside, or the severe cold of the northern mountains, may never permit the successions to reach this association. They are often held back by fire. When an oak woodland is severely burned over and no humus remains, nature courageously starts again with a group of open field plants. When pines are cut down, nature accommodates herself to this change in the environment and the conditions are such that gray birches can develop.

The harbingers of the new association and remnants of the old meet. Groups of birches spring up amid the junipers. Groups of old pines are found remaining among the oaks, or the oaks show their slender trunks in the midst of the pine forest.

The evidence of such transition is not found in the trees and shrubs alone. The flowers bear testimony by carrying their pictures from association to association. Aster novæ-angliæ, for instance, is found, if there is sufficient sun, in the open field, with the junipers, and under the slight shade of the birches.

The ever-changing topography of the land, too, has its influence. The gradual filling up of the ponds causes the changes in the location of the submerged, floating and emergent aquatic plants, for each requires

[6]

a certain depth of water for its best development. The
gradual deepening of the ravine has its influence upon
plants that grow there.   Only those which can adapt
themselves to the increasing shade and coolness sur-
vive.

Many an extensive area, with sweeping acreage
and varying topography, is a natural setting for a
country house. The fields and meadows, the woods,
the streams, ponds and ravines about it can bring
together all the different plant associations, for they
adjoin one another and intermingle. Property lines
may enclose a less varied scene and be limited to a
single association. The pines around the Adirondack
lakes offer an example, where every tree and every
partridge vine can be retained and the building hidden
in the shelter of the great trees can become an integral
part of the forest. There are other scenes which make
settings for summer cottages, winter lodges, for all-
year-round homes, such as the mountains of Pennsylvania with their hemlocks and rhododendrons, the
beech slopes of Vermont, the juniper hillsides of Connecticut, the rocky coasts of Maine and Massachusetts, the seaside of New Jersey, and the dunes of
Long Island. They may be retained in their full
beauty, with all of their individual characteristics.
Sometimes this is a problem of preservation, sometimes it is a matter of adding to and completing the
existing scenes.

A site of even an acre or less has many possibilities.
A small house may stand on a slope at the fringe of
the woods, with picturesque hedgerows around it,

with gray birches near it, and with a brook below. A still smaller property has the opportunity of being true to its environment. Its location within a well-defined area is often the key for the preservation of plants which belong there. A single oak can be taken as a guide. An appropriate selection can then be made of the shrubs and flowers that are associated with such a tree. This garden may have to be in miniature, but it can have delightful details and the verity of the natural landscape.

This study of native plants in relation to their environment brings out the fundamental principles upon which the indigenous vegetation is established, and the contribution that an understanding of these facts can make in the retention or recreation of the natural landscape. It draws attention, moreover, to the significance of retaining the original contours, and the adaptation of a house and garden to the lay of the land and to the spirit of the natural landscape.

CHAPTER II

THE OPEN FIELD

EACH uncultivated field or meadow is a natural garden covered over with many different kinds of flowers gathered together in lavish numbers. It is this wealth of plants that the farmer struggles against when he sows his grasslands. Because of them he has to till year after year. As soon as he stops they immediately begin to reëstablish themselves and in a few years come back into their own.

All of these flowers thrive in the open fields. They are controlled, however, by varying conditions of soil and moisture. Some are found only on rocky outcrops and in thin soil; some in rich well-drained areas and some in moist places. In any fair-sized acreage these situations adjoin one another and their characteristic vegetation becomes intermingled.

Some of these field flowers are well known and used in gardens. A few have found such favor in Europe that they have been extensively hybridized and reintroduced into this country as foreign varieties. Many of them, however, are still comparatively unknown. To really get acquainted with them, it is not enough to plant them in garden borders. They must be assembled as they are naturally assembled in the fields.

[9]

And to really recreate this natural field garden, it is important to keep the wide sunlit openness and the characteristic contours, to rehabilitate the enclosing hedgerows, to define the spontaneous paths as well as to reëstablish the all-over pattern of its flowers.

It is well to start by sowing it with clovers of which there are many different kinds, including white clover, *Trifolium repens,* the yellow clover, *Trifolium agrarium,* the rabbit-foot clover, *Trifolium arvense,* and many others. Some of these, to be sure, have been introduced from Europe and have become naturalized. They have a utilitarian purpose, for they keep out the weeds. The real reason for planting them is, however, because their soft green foliage and their little heads of vari-colored flowers make a delightful groundwork into which an embroidery of other plants can be worked. Besides the clovers, many kinds of grasses should also be grown for the graceful manner in which they combine with the flowers, and masses of hay-scented ferns can be planted for their light-filled yellow green.

Then, violets can be planted thickly everywhere— *Viola fimbriatula,* whose flowers grow on tall leafless stems. With them, buttercups can be mingled. *Ranunculus bulbosus,* the bulbous buttercup, and *Ranunculus fascicularis,* often called the early crowfoot, are for dry places, while *Ranunculus septentrionalis,* the swamp buttercup, is suitable for moist ground as its name implies. The flowers of the bulbous buttercup hug the ground. The others have stems that rise airily from thickly clustered foliage that make them seem like spots of gold amid the green. It is the way in which the flowers are scattered all over the field that makes their glistening effectiveness.

The robin's plantain and the painted cup flower at about this time. The robin's plantain has lavender-white, mauve or pink blossoms whose effect is very soft and fluffy, while the painted cup, with its scarlet-tipped, orange flowers, is startlingly brilliant when they flood a particularly moist place.

The yellow rocket, the ox-eye daisy, the blue chicory and the carrot, for all that they are such familiars of the fields, should not be used for they are really naturalized Europeans. There are many native flowers to use instead: masses of lupines with striking blue spikes; many native flags, *Iris versicolor,* with delicately formed slender flowers and effective sheath-like leaves; scattered groups of satiny gold evening primroses, *Œnothera biennis;* vivid expanses of burnt-orange butterfly weed; lavish clumps of yellow lilies; drifts of blue vervain; delicately sprinkled mauve beard-tongue, not to mention the golden-rods and asters.

These flowers make an all-over pattern. Other flowers can be used to edge the winding paths that wander unobtrusively through the fields. Among these are silvery white everlastings, chickweeds with starry blossoms and fine matted foliage, *Veronica officinalis* with luxuriant light green mats and blue flowers which may also be planted between the stepping stones. Pennyroyal, *Prunella vulgaris,* the heal-all, and little groups of *Polygala verticillata* with purple-tinged flowers can be planted here and there. The little yellow star grass and the blue-eyed grass can be put in special little spots to accentuate their daintiness.

On the other hand, there can be bluets in great numbers. Seen at a distance they sometimes look like a soft blue haze and then again they are so gray-white that they are like cobwebs spread upon the grass. At nearer view each little plant has a rare dignity and every little tubular flower a charming distinction. They can be planted along any part of the path, except where it is very dry. There the potentillas or cinquefoils can take their place. The potentillas grow in luxuriant masses and have many little glistening yellow flowers that seem like diminutive strawberry blossoms.

The prickly pear, *Opuntia vulgaris,* too, is good for very dry places. This picturesque cactus-like plant is usually seen growing singly or in clumps. And the pale corydalis, *Corydalis sempervirens,* grows naturally where it can silhouette its delicate stems and exquisitely yellow and pink tinted flowers against rocks.

There are many taller flowers, too, that can be planted in back of the low ones. The lespedezas or bush clovers with long flower spikes on rigid stems and *Pentstemon hirsutus,* with slender spires hung with tubular purplish flowers, can be used singly here and there. The milkweeds or asclepias, too, are most effective when they are singled out. There are two kinds: the blunt-leaved *Asclepias amplexicaulis* with greenish purple flowers and delicate long pods, and

Asclepias syriaca, the common milkweed, with heliotrope flowers arranged on top of great fleshy, deep green leaves.

On the other hand, the wild bergamot, *Monarda fistulosa,* with fringed corollas of lilac mauve, and *Lobelia syphilitica* with white-throated blue flowers, can be planted in scattered clumps. Of the several hypericums or St. John's-wort, with clusters of starry yellow flowers, only one is native. All of the several different loosestrifes have a delightful delicacy of habit, especially *Lysimachia quadrifolia,* with its group of four dark-streaked flowers modestly drooping beneath every whorl of light green leaves, and *Lysimachia terrestris,* with many little bronze-filled yellow blossoms arranged closely together upon a slender spike that stands erect and candle-like above the slender foliage.

All the violets and buttercups, the lupines and irises, the vervains and gerardias, can be gathered in small clumps and planted close to the path. The lilies, too, should be brought near it so that the details of their rich reddish-orange flowers with purple spottings can be fully appreciated. The flowers of *Lilium philadelphicum* that stand upright and alone upon an erect leaf-whorled stem look like carved ornaments, while *Lilium canadense,* with groups of nodding flowers, are even more exquisitely modeled.

Not only the paths can be bordered with these flowers. The hedgerows, too, can be filled with them. And besides the ones mentioned there are still others like the pink dogbane, the white vervain and the meadow rue. The golden-rods and asters can also be gathered together there. They must be kept under control, however, for they spread so rapidly that they would soon usurp the entire field if they were permitted, as they so often actually do.

Both golden-rods and asters are fascinating in themselves, in the number of their species and in the luxuriousness of their effects. Of the asters, the most familiar is the *Aster novæ-angliæ* that grows everywhere. It has a stout, stiff, hairy stem topped with large clusters of brilliant violet flowers. There is *Aster lateriflorus,* whose slender-leaved stems are terminated with lavender flowers. There is *Aster macrophyllus,* with flat-topped flower heads of lavender violet and the deep blue *Aster patens* with widely-spaced rays that give it a very delicate effect. There is *Aster lævis* with light blue flowers daintily arranged upon slender stems, *Aster prenanthoides,* with deep violet flowers that are sharply serrated, and *Aster cordifolius.* Besides, there are several white ones, the tall white *Aster paniculatus* with sparse flowers and long slender leaves, *Aster ptarmicoides,* the white aster with yarrow-like heads of small flowers and lanceolate foliage, *Aster vimineus* with slender sprays of tiny flowers, *Aster divaricatus,* and *Aster ericoides.* These various species succeed one another in blooming from August to November. The last to hold its flowers is the *Aster ericoides.*

It is not only necessary that all the flowers be in the field. It is also important to consider the boundaries. The rail fences, the stone walls and the hedgerows are the characteristic enclosures. They divide the fields from one another and separate them from the lanes and roads.

The hedgerow is a comparatively narrow planting strip which the farmer did not encroach upon in clearing for his arable fields. Its edges are usually straight and well ordered. If the outline is at all irregular it is because a rocky outcrop made it impossible for the plow to reach it. The hedgerow has a delightful picturesqueness. Some of its spontaneity is due to the varying ages of the plants, for the seedling growth is constantly springing up around maturer vegetation, but its character depends for the most part upon the manner in which each plant in it adapts itself.

Cornus paniculata, the dogwood, is one of its prominent shrubs, in dry places, because it is able to adjust itself admirably to poor soil and lack of moisture. It generally grows all by itself and forms veritable hedge-like formations. The bushes are so beautifully formed into undulating masses that they have an air of choiceness. They are noticeable in the spring when the young leaves have a bronze tone and the flowers are cream-toned. They are equally effective in midsummer when cool white berries show on cerise pedicels amid the green foliage. *Cornus circinata,* sometimes found with the panicled dogwoods, is not quite as well equipped for its position and always remains a minor note in the planting. On the other hand, the chokecherries and the pin cherries adapt themselves so readily to almost every condition that they are almost always to be found. They are most

delightful when they seem to spring up quite care-
lessly here and there amid the other shrubs. Their
graceful habits lighten the effect of the planting. The
drooping racemes of the one and the umbel-like clusters of the other make them particularly pleasing
during the spring. Of the two the chokecherry is the
lovelier. It is well worth the effort to keep it free
from its special pest, the tent caterpillar. If it is
watched early enough in the year the burden of care
is not overwhelming.

Viburnum prunifolium abounds, also, in hedgerows.
Its striking habit and handsome foliage make it one
of the most beautiful shrubs. It is especially noticeable in May when every horizontal branch bears large
cymes of cream-white flowers. It is often found
singly, sometimes at almost stated intervals. Then it
forms a kind of repeat pattern. Sometimes, spreading as it does by underground stolons, it makes sturdy
groups that occasionally grow into great masses. It
is always surprising that such a precious-looking
shrub should grow best in the thinnest of soils and in
the most difficult places. In the same situations are
scattered, too, groups of *Viburnum pubescens* and
Viburnum Lentago, occasional scrub oaks and abundant masses of sweet ferns and wild roses.

In moister places there are hazelnuts, *Viburnum
dentatum* and *Viburnum cassinoides,* with *Spiræa
latifolia,* the meadow-sweet, and *Spiræa tomentosa,*
the steeple bush, and *Potentilla fruticosa,* the shrubby
cinquefoil, to fill in the foreground.

The hazelnuts have rugged stems, rough foliage,

[16]

brown scaly buds with coral-tongued pistils, and ornamental fruits that make them very decorative throughout the year. Sometimes they grow in thickets, and
then again they appear in smaller groups among the
viburnums. *Viburnum dentatum,* the arrow-wood,
is a sturdy shrub with rugged, strongly-veined foliage. *Viburnum cassinoides,* the wild raisin, seems
more delicate. It is smaller, hardly more than six feet
high, with graceful low branches and shining foliage.
Its soft white flowers are arranged in small umbels.
Its fruit is particularly fascinating. It becomes noticeable in August when it is greenish white. By Sep-
tember it has turned turquoise blue. In October it is
rose pink with occasional cymes that have all three
colors intermingled. Finally before it falls, it turns
blue black.

The viburnums and dogwoods, the hazels and chokecherries are much the same height. Variety is gained
however, through the distinctive individuality of their
stemmage and color as shown in the stiff, erect twigs
of the gray-toned *Cornus paniculata,* in the limpid
character of *Viburnum Lentago,* in the definiteness of
the *Viburnum dentatum* growth, and in the angularity
of the *Viburnum prunifolium* branching.

In addition to this, small trees like *Prunus serotina,*
the wild black cherry, *Prunus nigra,* and cratægus in
numerous species, often outstrip the shrubs in height
and contribute a modest irregularity to the skyline of
the hedgerow. This variation is further accentuated
by the vines that tumble over the stone walls and
fences in tangled masses and clamber even into shrub

and tree in luxuriant festoons. There are honey-suckles that have fiery red flowers, Virginia creepers that are very showy when the autumn turns the foli-age flame color, and bitter-sweets that become con-spicuous when their berries turn orange and then open to show their scarlet centers. Besides, there are two kinds of wild grapes with fragrant flowers, soft brownish-red spring foliage, and luxuriant, wonder-fully formed summer leaves. *Vitis lubrusca,* the fox grape, is an ancestor of our familiar Concord and adapts itself to every situation. Its leaves are very large and opposite each one is a fascinating tendril. The fruit is sometimes amber and sometimes purple. *Vitis æstivalis,* the summer grape, prefers moist places. Its leaves are smaller, more lobed and dis-tinctly pubescent underneath. Its fruit is black with a bloom.

Hedgerows like these are sometimes found full grown and then again they have to be entirely recreated. They can border the roads and drives. They can be brought close to the house for groups of any one of their shrubs, trees and vines are appropri-ate against it. They are, moreover, essential for the enclosure of the field.

Hedgerows emphasize the fact that a field of this kind requires a country setting. It needs an acre or so at the outskirts of the town, or better still, a larger acreage farther out, to give it the proper dimensions. It needs country surroundings with encircling hills that are well wooded and a stream that flows through the valley. It needs, too, a country house that is in

The Open Field

spirit with it. Such a house should have the architectural simplicity of a farmstead, especially of the early American type. Sometimes the house can be really an old one. Sometimes, it is freshly designed in the old manner with low and broad-stretched lines, with roofs and gables that fit the rolling topography, and with wide terraces. Often a great old tree shelters it and throws its shadows across it. Out beyond in the sunshine the fields can then be one luxurious mass of flowers.

THE OPEN FIELD ASSOCIATION

In all lists plants with * are not native, but have become so well established that they have been included in the lists.

SHRUBS

Celastrus scandens .... Bitter-sweet
Cornus circinata .... Round-leaved Dogwood
Cornus paniculata .... Dogwood
Corylus americana .... Hazelnut
Crataegus sp. .... Hawthorn
Juniperus communis .... Ground Juniper
Lonicera sempervirens .... Trumpet Honeysuckle
Lyonia ligustrina .... Male Berry
Myrica asplenifolia .... Sweet Fern
Potentilla fruticosa .... Shrubby Cinquefoil
Prunus cuneata .... Plum
Prunus nigra .... Canada Plum
Prunus pennsylvanica .... Pin Cherry
Prunus serotina .... Wild Black Cherry
Prunus virginiana .... Choke Cherry
Psedera quinquefolia .... Virginia Creeper
Quercus illicifolia .... Scrub Oak
Rhus copallina .... Dwarf Sumach
Rhus glabra .... Smooth Sumach
Rhus typhina .... Staghorn Sumach
Ribes vulgare * .... Red Currant
Robinia hispida .... Rose Acacia
Rosa blanda .... Rose
Rosa rubiginosa * .... Sweetbrier Rose
Rubus allegheniensis .... Blackberry
Rubus idaeus * .... Raspberry
Rubus recurvans .... Blackberry

SHRUBS (*Continued*)

Rubus villosus ....Dewberry
Spiræa latifolia ....Meadow-sweet
Spiræa tomentosa ....Steeple Bush
Viburnum cassinoides ....Wild Raisin
Viburnum dentatum ....Arrow-wood
Viburnum Lentago ....Nannyberry
Viburnum prunifolium ....Black Haw
Viburnum pubescens ....Downy Arrow-wood
Vitis æstivalis ....Summer Grape
Vitis labrusca ....Northern Fox Grape
Zanthoxylum americanum ....Prickly Ash

HERBS

Achillea Millefolium ....Yarrow
Anaphalis margaritacea * ....Pearly Everlasting
Anemone canadensis ....Anemone
Anemone virginiana ....Anemone
Antennaria neglecta ....Everlasting
Antennaria neodioica ....Everlasting
Antennaria Parlinii ....Everlasting
Antennaria plantaginifolia ....Plantain-leaved Everlasting
Apocynum androsaemifolium ....Spreading Dogbane
Apocynum cannabinum ....Indian Hemp
Arenaria lateriflora ....Sandwort
Asclepias amplexicaulis ....Milkweed
Asclepias syriaca ....Common Milkweed
Asclepias tuberosa ....Butterfly Weed
Asparagus officinalis * ....Asparagus
Asperula galioides * ....Asperula
Aster cordifolius ....Aster
Aster divaricatus ....Aster
Aster ericoides ....Aster
Aster lævis ....Aster
Aster lateriflorus ....Aster
Aster macrophyllus ....Aster
Aster novæ-angliæ ....Aster
Aster paniculatus ....Aster
Aster patens ....Aster
Aster prenanthoides ....Aster
Aster ptarmicoides ....Aster
Aster vimineus ....Aster
Barbarea vulgaris * ....Yellow Rocket
Blephilia ciliata ....Blephilia
Campanula rapunculoides * ....Bellflower
Castilleja coccinea ....Scarlet Painted Cup
Centaurea nigra * ....Spanish Buttons

The Open Field

Cerastium vulgatum *	Common Mouse-ear Chickweed
Cerastium arvense *	Field Mouse-ear Chickweed
Chrysanthemum Leucanthemum *	Ox-eye Daisy
Cichorium Intybus *	Chicory
Cirsium lanceolatum *	Bull Thistle
Convolvulus spithamæus	Bindweed
Coronilla varia *	Coronilla
Corydalis sempervirens	Pale Corydalis
Cuphea petiolata	Clammy Cuphea
Daucus Carota *	Carrot
Dianthus Armeria *	Deptford Pink
Dioscorea villosa	Wild Yam-root
Dipsacus sylvestris *	Wild Teasel
Epilobium augustifolium	Fireweed
Erigeron annuus	Daisy Fleabane
Erigeron philadelphicus	Fleabane
Erigeron pulchellus	Robin's Plantain
Fragaria virginiana	Strawberry
Galium Mollugo *	Bedstraw
Gnaphalium polycephalum	Common Everlasting
Gnaphalium uliginosum	Low Cudweed
Hedeoma pulegioides	American Pennyroyal
Helianthus divaricatus	Sunflower
Hieracium aurantiacum *	Devil's Paint-brush
Hieracium florentinum *	King Devil
Hieracium Gronovii	Hawkweed
Hieracium Pilosella *	Mouse-ear
Houstonia cærulea	Bluets
Hypericum canadense	St. John's-wort
Hypericum perforatum *	Common St. John's-wort
Hypoxis hirsuta	Star Grass
Iris versicolor	Larger Blue Flag
Lespedeza capitata	Bush Clover
Lespedeza simulata	Bush Clover
Lilium canadense	Wild Yellow Lily
Lilium philadelphicum	Wood Lily
Linaria vulgaris *	Butter and Eggs
Lobelia inflata	Indian Tobacco
Lobelia siphilitica	Great Lobelia
Lobelia spicata	Lobelia
Lupinus perennis	Wild Lupine
Lychnis alba *	White Campion
Lysimachia quadrifolia	Loosestrife
Lysimachia terrestris	Loosestrife
Medicago falcata *	Medick
Medicago sativa *	Alfalfa
Melilotus officinalis *	Yellow Melilot

American Plants for American Gardens

HERBS (*Continued*)

Monarda fistulosa	Wild Bergamot
Oenothera biennis	Common Evening Primrose
Oenothera fruticosa	Sundrops
Oenothera pumila	Evening Primrose
Origanum vulgare *	Wild Marjoram
Opuntia vulgaris	Prickly Pear
Oxalis filipes	Wood Sorrel
Oxalis stricta	Wood Sorrel
Pentstemon hirsutus	Beard-tongue
Phaseolus polystachyus	Wild Bean
Physalis pruinosa	Strawberry Tomato
Phytolacca decandra	Common Poke
Plantago lanceolata *	Rib Grass
Plantago major	Common Plantain
Polygala sanguinea	Milkwort
Polygala verticillata	Whorled Milkwort
Polygonum virginianum	Knotweed
Potentilla arguta	Cinquefoil
Potentilla canadensis	Cinquefoil
Potentilla intermedia *	Cinquefoil
Potentilla pumila	Cinquefoil
Potentilla recta *	Rough Fruited Cinquefoil
Prunella vulgaris	Heal-all
Pycnanthemum flexuosum	Mountain Mint
Pycnanthemum virginianum	Mountain Mint
Ranunculus bulbosus *	Bulbous Buttercup
Ranunculus fascicularis	Early Crowfoot
Ranunculus septentrionalis	Swamp Buttercup
Rudbeckia hirta	Black-eyed Susan
Rumex Acetosella *	Sheep Sorrel
Saponaria officinalis *	Bouncing Bet
Satureja vulgaris	Basil
Silene latifolia *	Bladder Campion
Silene noctiflora *	Night-flowering Catchfly
Sisyrinchium angustifolium	Blue-eyed Grass
Solanum nigrum	Common Nightshade
Solidago altissima	Golden-rod
Solidago bicolor	Golden-rod
Solidago canadensis	Golden-rod
Solidago graminifolia	Golden-rod
Solidago nemoralis	Golden-rod
Solidago rigida	Golden-rod
Solidago rugosa	Golden-rod
Solidago rugosa var. *villosa*	Golden-rod
Specularia perfoliata	Venus' Looking Glass
Stachys arenicola	Hedge Nettle
Stellaria longifolia	Common Chickweed

The Open Field

Stellaria media* .... Chickweed
Steironema ciliatum .... Steironema
Tanacetum vulgare* .... Common Tansy
Taraxacum officinale* .... Common Dandelion
Thalictrum polygamum .... Tall Meadow Rue
Tragopogon pratensis* .... Goat's Beard
Trichostema dichotomum .... Bastard Pennyroyal
Trifolium agrarium* .... Yellow Clover
Trifolium arense* .... Rabbit-foot Clover
Trifolium hybridum* .... Alsike Clover
Trifolium pratense* .... Red Clover
Trifolium procumbens* .... Low Hop Clover
Trifolium repens .... White Clover
Verbascum Blattaria* .... Moth Mullein
Verbascum Thapsus* .... Common Mullein
Verbena urticæfolia .... White Vervain
Veronica officinalis .... Common Speedwell
Vicia villosa* .... Winter Vetch
Viola fimbriatula .... Violet
Waldsteinia fragarioides .... Barren Strawberry

FERNS

Dicksonia punctilobula .... Hay-scented Fern

CHAPTER III

THE dry sunny hillside is so rocky and exposed that only a few plants are able to adapt themselves to its rigorous conditions. Among them the red cedar, *Juniperus virginiana,* is the most prominent. They scatter over the hillside; they crown the knolls; they mount the slopes in groups of varying numbers; they assemble on the ridges in long, closely gathered masses. They are always striking in form. As young trees they are slender and columnar and branched to the very ground. As old specimens they are loose-limbed and broadly conical with a strong brown trunk showing below wide up-curving branches. They stand out as picturesque silhouettes against the rocky hillside or show their jagged outlines against the sky. And because these junipers are so telling in form and so impressive in numbers, all the plants that grow about them are known as members of the Juniper Association.

The ground juniper, *Juniperus communis,* is one of them. It is in marked contrast to the cedar. It is a flat and matted shrub with upturned bristly branches. It grows singly or in masses that are spaced far apart.

[24]

The Juniper Hillside

The black haw, *Viburnum prunifolium,* grows in small groups close against the cedars. It has a strong angular habit and horizontal branching. The scrub oak and the choke cherry are found here and there. And roses, sweet fern, bayberry and blueberry cover the fields and drift downward into the hollows. The sumachs, too, gather in wide-flung masses in the lower and less sterile spots. Besides, bittersweet and Virginia creeper climb into trees and shrubs, tumble over rocks and clamber over stone walls. And the common barberry, *Berberis vulgaris,* grows there singly or in small clumps. It is really a European variety, introduced years ago, that found this situation so congenial that it became naturalized.

It is the junipers, gray-toned in spring and deeper green later on, that make the foil for the seasonal effects of these shrubs and vines. Their evergreen sets off the black haw when the numerous sprays of white flowers make the one telling flower display of this association. And they make a background for the striking colors that the autumn brings. The black haw foliage turns wine-red then. The Virginia creeper is flame-colored. The bittersweet berries are bright orange-yellow. The leaves of the sumachs make crimson splashes and their velvety fruits are mahogany-red spires. And the junipers themselves have turquoise-blue berries.

The irregular spaces of seemingly barren ground between the juniper groups and the shrub masses are covered with low herbaceous plants. The outcropping ledges are veritable little rock gardens. Mosses and

[25]

lichens spread them with soft grays and greens. Tiny rare maidenhair spleenworts and other small evergreen ferns spring up in many a little nook. The gray rosettes of saxifrages fill every crevice, while the slender stems of the airy columbines rise delicately above their groundwork. These make choice little pictures. The sunny stretches, on the other hand, have different plants. First come the bulbous buttercups and *Viola fimbriatula,* all gold and blue in the springtime. Next come the yellow and white *Linaria vulgaris,* butter and eggs, surprisingly rare-looking in this setting, and the delicate maroon-touched moth mullein, as dainty as can be. These are really naturalized, but they have long ago become as necessary a detail to the scene as any of the flowers that are truly indigenous. Then, there are pennyroyal and evening primroses, mountain mints and speedwell, St. John's-wort and bush clover, common yarrow and black-eyed Susans. Later, the goldenrods are in flower; *Solidago graminifolia, Solidago nemoralis* and *Solidago rugosa* var. *villosa.* They have graceful sprays and dainty flower chains. And with the goldenrods come the asters. *Aster cordifolius* and *Aster prenanthoides* have blue flowers. *Aster vimineus* has small white flowers, and the white slender-sprayed *Aster ericoides* is the daintiest of them all. This intermingled white and gold and blue is scattered lightly over the uneven fields and lasts for several weeks. And, as it fades, the silvery-white everlastings show against the browned autumn-dried flowers and the fawn-colored grasses.

The Juniper Hillside

All of these trees and shrubs, vines, flowers and ferns are sturdy plants. They withstand drastic changes of temperature. They brave poor soil and excessive dryness. They endure windswept exposure. They win out over every adverse condition. But more than this, they adapt themselves with telling informality to the irregular topography, perfect the ruggedness of the environment and vitalize the rock contours.

Such a hillside stands in rugged picturesqueness above the lowlands with their fields and streams. It is in strong contrast to the gray birch copses, to the oak woods and to the pines around it. The very thought of owning it and of keeping it unspoiled is stimulating. Unfortunately, in the course of time and circumstance, the plow may have uprooted many of the shrubs and flowers, and the ax cut away the trees. If that is so, there is a marvelous incentive to recreate what has been destroyed. And if all the plants of a particular hillside have been cleared away, other existing examples can become inspiring guides for their reproduction.

The size of the property matters very little, for the juniper association can adapt itself equally well to large and small places. Its assemblings can be repeated in infinite variety on a large estate, and yet the plants are so few in number that its arrangements are also adapted to limited surroundings, to even the smallest property.

Such a hillside is full of possibilities when it becomes the site for a house. It can influence the style and can control the shape, the roof lines, the plan and the materials. In this way, the building becomes one with its surroundings. Under the sway of the rugged picturesqueness, the house becomes low and wide-spread so that it nestles into the hillside. Its outlines are irregular so that the wings and ells fit the uneven slope. The roof has gables and over-hanging eaves that seem to repeat the contours. The first floor is arranged on several levels to conform to the topography. And the materials of the house are suggested by the environment. Dark brown shingles can blend with the green of the cedars, stucco can take its tone from the color of the ledges, stone can be hewn from the rocks themselves.

Such a house becomes an actual part of the landscape when its immediate surroundings are also adapted to the topography of the juniper hillside and when the planting plan is developed with the materials that naturally grow there. As soon as the plan is begun, some of the possibilities manifest themselves. Take the drive. It can be adapted to the contours and made to wind naturally up the hill. Its whole way can be outlined with irregular clumps of cedars and the turns marked by groups of black haws. All along the edges masses of blueberries and roses can be planted in broad borders. These plants can surround the turn-around that is sunk inconspicuously into a hollow. They can be brought up to the house itself and arranged against it. The black haw has such an impressive structure that it can be very effective beside the entrance door. The scrub oaks, difficult though they are to transplant, are worth a trial because their irregular forms are so striking against the wall. The cherries make an excellent group for the corner of the house where they can best display their shining foliage and their hanging racemes of white flowers. The roses are low enough to be placed under the windows and the little cinquefoils can make a green ground cover for the shrubs and spread their trailers out to the edge of the drive.

In developing the surroundings of the house for outdoor living, some of the most interesting possibilities of the juniper hillside can be realized. Due to the irregular contours, a series of little outdoor places can be built at different levels. Some can be raised a little above the surroundings while others can be sunk cozily into the slope. Dry-laid walls and rugged steps can be built to connect them in an informal manner. The native plant material adapts itself to them all. One little place can be well-sheltered from the wind by masses of enclosing cedars and Virginia creepers can trail over the walls. Another place that is hollowed out of the hill can become a shady court. On the top of its walls common juniper can make a green border and bittersweet cover the wall with hanging streamers. The fruit of the bittersweet is so effective that it attracts the attention of everyone, but its little greenish flowers that are arranged in lovely racemes-like clusters are overlooked except by the observant few.

And there is always need for a terrace. It should

be close to the living-room so that it can be used at any time and at any season. It should be made dry underfoot by well-laid paving while mosses and lichens can be brought in to cover the flags and fill the crevices between. Their matted growth makes a soft floor-covering. A low retaining wall can be built around it. At the base of this wall a narrow border can be filled with evergreen ferns, a mass of polypods with here and there a taller Christmas fern. This wall can be laid without mortar. The earth that binds the stone together can then be filled with tiny spleen-wort ferns and with the small polypods as a green background for the gray saxifrages and the silvery white everlastings that can be made to peep out of the wall. Columbines can be tucked into soil pockets everywhere in incredible numbers. They are such lacy plants with their gray-green fern-like leaves and this daintiness is heightened by the way their red and yellow flowers nod on slender stems. Their delightful flowering is followed in the autumn by new rosettes that cover the wall after the far-flung seeds have taken hold in every little crevice of their own accord. This will make a wall garden of unusual delicacy.

The steps of this terrace can lead to a path that is made to wander leisurely through flowers. It can be bordered all along its way with violets and bulbous buttercups. Even after the flowers are gone, their evergreen rosettes make a lasting ground cover. They can be intermingled to edge borders filled with fragrant mints and pennyroyals and surrounded with masses of sweet fern. This makes a garden of rare sweet scent. The path can then wander on through other intermingled flowers that spread out in all directions. The autumn effects can be especially interesting when the asters and goldenrods come in bloom with occasional bush clovers rising up among them. For all their gay profusion, they have a rugged refinement which is characteristic of all the flowers that grow in barren soil upon open and wind-dried hillsides.

These naturalistic flower gardens can be surrounded with blueberry bushes. They are lovely shrubs, full of interest through the year. In the spring clusters of white bell-flowers come before the leaves. These are followed later on by sweet blueberries that ripen in the midst of smooth green foliage. In the autumn the leaves turn to a bronze that takes on varied tones with refraction of the sunlight from their shining surfaces. Even in winter the angular branches and the interlaced twigs are charmingly accented by plump little reddish buds.

These low shrubs cover the ground and can be made to drift off to boundaries of cherries and scrub oaks. The viburnums and sumachs can be made telling by adding clumps of cedars. It is planting of this kind that can blend the house and its immediate surroundings imperceptibly with the natural landscape.

American Plants for American Gardens

THE JUNIPER ASSOCIATION

TREES

Juniperus virginiana	Red Cedar
Robinia Pseudo-Acacia	Common Locust

SHRUBS

Berberis vulgaris *	Common Barberry
Celastrus scandens	Bittersweet
Cornus paniculata	Dogwood
Juniperus communis	Common Juniper
Lonicera sempervirens	Trumpet Honeysuckle
Myrica asplenifolia	Sweet Fern
Myrica carolinensis	Bayberry
Prunus virginiana	Choke Cherry
Psedera quinquefolia	Virginia Creeper
Quercus ilicifolia	Scrub Oak
Rhus copallina	Dwarf Sumach
Rhus glabra	Smooth Sumach
Rhus typhina	Staghorn Sumach
Ribes vulgare *	Red Currant
Rosa blanda	Rose
Rosa rubiginosa *	Sweetbrier Rose
Rubus allegheniensis	Blackberry
Rubus idæus	Raspberry
Rubus recurvans	Blackberry
Rubus villosus	Dewberry
Vaccinium pennsylvanicum	Low Sweet Blueberry
Viburnum cassinoides	Wild Raisin
Viburnum dentatum	Arrow-wood
Viburnum Lentago	Nannyberry
Viburnum prunifolium	Black Haw
Viburnum pubescens	Downy Arrow-wood
Zanthoxylum americanum	Prickly Ash

HERBS

Achillea Millefolium	Common Yarrow
Anaphalis margaritacea	Pearly Everlasting
Anemonella thalictroides	Rue Anemone
Antennaria neglecta	Everlasting
Antennaria neodioica	Everlasting
Antennaria Parlinii	Everlasting
Antennaria plantaginifolia	Plantain-leaved Everlasting
Aquilegia canadensis	Wild Columbine
Aster cordifolius	Aster
Aster ericoides	Aster
Aster novæ-angliæ	Aster

[32]

The Juniper Hillside

HERBS (Continued)

Aster prenanthoides .... Aster
Aster vimineus .... Small White Aster
Blephilia ciliata .... Blephilia
Cerastium vulgatum .... Mouse-ear Chickweed
Chimaphila maculata .... Spotted Wintergreen
Chimaphila umbellata .... Pipsissewa
Chrysanthemum Leucanthemum* ...... Ox-eye Daisy
Comandra umbellata .... Bastard Toad-flax
Desmodium nudiflorum .... Tick Trefoil
Gnaphalium polycephalum .... Cudweed
Gnaphalium uliginosum .... Low Cudweed
Hedeoma pulegioides .... American Pennyroyal
Hieracium aurantiacum* .... Devil's Paint Brush
Hypericum canadense .... St. John's-wort
Lespedeza capitata .... Bush Clover
Lespedeza simulata .... Bush Clover
Linaria vulgaris* .... Butter and Eggs
Luzula parviflora .... Wood Rush
Mitchella repens .... Partridge Berry
Monarda fistulosa .... Wild Bergamot
Monarda punctata .... Horse Mint
Œnothera biennis .... Common Evening Primrose
Œnothera fruticosa .... Sundrops
Œnothera pumila .... Evening Primrose
Oxalis filipes .... Wood Sorrel
Oxalis stricta .... Wood Sorrel
Plantago lanceolata* .... Rib Grass
Polygala pauciflora .... Fringed Polygala
Polygonatum biflorum .... Small Solomon's Seal
Potentilla argentea .... Silvery Cinquefoil
Potentilla canadensis .... Cinquefoil
Potentilla pumila .... Cinquefoil
Prunella vulgaris .... Self-heal
Pycnanthemum flexuosum .... Mountain Mint
Pycnanthemum virginianum .... Mountain Mint
Pyrola chlorantha .... Shin Leaf
Pyrola elliptica .... Shin Leaf
Ranunculus acris* .... Tall Buttercup
Ranunculus bulbosus* .... Bulbous Buttercup
Ranunculus fascicularis .... Early Crowfoot
Rudbeckia hirta .... Black-eyed Susan
Saxifraga virginiensis .... Early Saxifrage
Smilacina racemosa .... False Solomon's Seal
Solidago bicolor .... Silver-rod
Solidago graminifolia .... Golden-rod
Solidago nemoralis .... Golden-rod
Solidago rugosa .... Golden-rod

[33]

American Plants for American Gardens

HERBS (Continued)

Solidago rugosa var. *villosa* .... Golden-rod
Stellaria media * .... Common Chickweed
Thalictrum dioicum .... Early Rue
Verbascum Blattaria * .... Moth Mullein
Veronica officinalis .... Speedwell
Viola fimbriatula .... Violet
Viola latiuscula .... Violet
Viola pubescens .... Downy Yellow Violet

FERNS

Aspidium marginale .... Shield Fern
Asplenium platyneuron .... Spleenwort
Asplenium Ruta-muraria .... Wall Rue
Asplenium Trichomanes .... Maidenhair Spleenwort
Lycopodium obscurum var. *dendroideum*. Club Moss
Polypodium vulgare .... Polypody
Polystichum acrostichoides .... Christmas Fern

CHAPTER IV

WHEREVER there are gray birches, Nature is in one of her lightest moods. These gray-white trees of slender form gather together in fairy-like groves. Their slim grace is accentuated by the way they often spring up in fives and sixes from a single root. When young they are gray-brown but later on they are phantom-white with black twigs and black notches. The effect is full of that mystery that etchings and delicate pencil drawings have. The gossamer quality is ever present; in the spring when their filmy foliage is light-filled, in summer when their green is soft, in autumn when it is all sun-lit yellow, and even in the winter when the trees take on again their keynote colors from the snow and dark earth.

The floor of these birch groves is spread with evergreen ferns, with luxurious Christmas ferns, with lacy shield ferns, with polypods gathered in delightful green mats and occasionally even with the spleenworts. The spring spreads the ground with the tiny yellow-blossomed vines of cinquefoils, with the white flowered strawberries, with creeping *Veronica officinalis,* with self-heals and with buttercups. And the

[35]

autumn brings the golden-rod, pearly everlasting and silvery-white aster into bloom.

Here is a scene of delightful simplicity. It can be easily recreated and becomes effective almost immediately. Gray birches are rapid growers and fair-sized trees can be moved without difficulty. It is always advisable to transplant them in the spring. It is safest to use dormant trees but they can be moved even after the new leaves are fairly well developed. This work must be done quickly, however, in fact within a few hours, so that the foliage does not have a chance to droop.

Gray birches are comparatively short-lived. It is, therefore, best to surround them with slower growing and more permanent trees. In nature, the gray birch copses protect the seedling white pines which grow up in their midst and supplant them.

Gray birches are found, too, in many different places and sometimes exist under difficult conditions. They group themselves along slow streams, around drought-enduring bogs, on dry exposed hillsides among cedars, and on the edge of woods and in the shelter of great trees. In such places they heighten the effect of all the other planting.

The delicate way in which gray birches envelop their settings make them especially desirable. On an extensive estate, masses of them can be left to outline the drive, to skirt a sedge-bordered pool, to surround a clearing, to make a sweeping border to a woods and to give a foreground to pines. They are, however, even more appropriate for a small place where they

can be gathered in a little grove about a small house. Their dainty habits accentuate the picturesqueness of little ells and one-storied wings, of casement windows and latticed porches, of gay colored shutters and door-ways. They are especially fitted, too, to edge little terraces, to encircle tiny lawns and to enclose small gardens. Polypods and tiny spleenworts and black-stemmed *Asplenium platyneuron* can be planted in the crevices of steps and in dry-laid walls. Christmas ferns can be used as borders. Cinquefoils and straw-berries can edge the paths with spontaneous irregu-larity. In among them clumps of self-heals and speedwells can be planted and in back of them there can be masses of buttercups, everlastings, silver-rods and asters. The daintiness of these flowers can be offset by clumps of shield ferns with their tall and graceful fronds. These spring and fall effects, as well as the summer greenness, is always heightened by the sunlight that loves to filter through gray birches and play upon the flower and fern covered ground.

THE GRAY BIRCH ASSOCIATION

TREES

Betula populifolia ....Gray Birch

HERBS

Anaphalis margaritacea ....Pearly Everlasting
Aster cordifolius ....Aster
Aster prenanthoides ....Aster
Aster vimineus ....Aster
Epigaea repens ....Mayflower
Fragaria virginiana ....Strawberry
Lespedeza capitata ....Bush Clover
Lespedeza simulata ....Bush Clover
Oxalis filipes ....Wood Sorrel
Oxalis stricta ....Wood Sorrel

[37]

American Plants for American Gardens

HERBS (Continued)

Potentilla canadensis ....Cinquefoil
Potentilla pumila ....Cinquefoil
Prunella vulgaris ....Self-heal
Ranunculus acris* ....Tall Buttercup
Ranunculus bulbosus* ....Bulbous Buttercup
Solidago bicolor ....Golden-rod
Veronica officinalis ....Common Speedwell

FERNS

Aspidium marginale ....Shield Fern
Asplenium platyneuron ....Spleenwort
Asplenium Trichomanes ....Spleenwort
Polypodium vulgare ....Polypody
Polystichum acrostichoides ....Christmas Fern

CHAPTER V

THE PINES

WHITE pines are lordly evergreens. Within the forest they have trunks of marvelous straightness that rise without side branches to a great height. The infinite repetition of the vertical lines expresses their stateliness. On the edge of the woods, however, the branches are stretched out horizontally in wide-spaced tiers that droop and sway with restful rhythm.

The weathered brown of the bark and the soft green of the foliage is repeated on the earth under the trees by the thick mat of dried needles and the many little ground-covers. There are partridge berries with tiny-leafed, tiny-berried vines. There are bunchberries with little dogwood-like blossoms and red fruit clusters. There are checkerberries that spread by creeping rootstocks into veritable carpets and hide frail little urn-shaped flowers and red berries beneath checkered leaves. There are club mosses with miniature tree-formed shoots and other lycopodiums with thick light-toned evergreen streamers. Evergreen ferns grow in masses. Marvelous lady's slippers are gathered together in colonies. And, here and there, pipissewas and pyrolas are scattered singly and show their daintily sculptured waxy flowers above evergreen leaves.

[39]

These low ground-covers and the pines above them are a small group that has reserve and dignity. Because the pine gives it its character the group is known as the Pine Association.

White pines grow on the sides of mountains, on the tops of high ridges, on rocky shores and beside crag-edged lakes. They begin to grow in gray birch woods where shade is provided for their seedlings and protection for the young trees. In particularly rugged spots, the white pine saplings gain foothold among pitch pines and rigorous red pines that establish themselves first. The intermingling of the three varieties brings out interesting differentiations in their bark textures and their needle lengths while the scraggy growth of the pitch pines and of the red pines is a foil for the grandeur of the white pines.

In the north, white pines still cover great areas and have been left undisturbed for centuries. Together with arbor-vitæ, spruce, balsam fir and hemlock they make a landscape rich in varied evergreens. Farther south they are seldom found now as great forests, but are usually seen in small woods, in groups and even as single specimens.

If the pines are young, softly rounded and bushy, it is evident that they are just beginning to establish themselves. In an old woods, however, they may be either sheltering very young oaks or struggling to hold their own in a mature oak woods that is supplanting them.

White pines deserve to be preserved or planted again. Seedlings are used in reforesting and come

The Pines

to their full grandeur only after a century, but fair-sized young trees can be planted on estates and in gardens and they develop, in a comparatively short time, at least some of the dignity of old trees. A few great trees, indeed a single aged pine, already on a property can be ever so valuable as a stately background for the house. The brown bark and the evergreen blend with weathered shingles or contrast well with brick and gray stone. And the wide-spread evergreen-laden branches with needles grouped together in slender clusters is a delightfully shady setting for a garden made up of all the ground-loving companions of the white pines. Bunchberries can outline its paths, partridge berries can make edgings for masses of ferns, checkerberries can be used as ground covers under pipsissewas and pyrolas, while lady's slippers can be planted at the foot of each tree. Such a garden is possible upon many a wooded slope or hilltop. It can be near the house, beside the very terrace or just beyond the living room, or it can be farther away from the house in a more secluded spot wherever a pine rises up above birches or among oaks.

In real forests of white pines, the entire scene can be simply kept intact with paths that are needle-covered, ground that is spread with green creepers, and views that are framed by tall trees. Log cabins and rough stone lodges can be built to fit into these surroundings. They can be low so as to accentuate the height of the trees. They can be inconspicuous, almost invisible even at a short distance, among the rocks and in the shadowy depth of the woods.

THE PINE ASSOCIATION

TREES

Pinus resinosa	Red Pine
Pinus rigida	Pitch Pine
Pinus Strobus	White Pine

HERBS

Chimaphila umbellata	Pipsissewa
Cornus canadensis	Bunchberry
Cypripedium acaule	Lady's Slipper
Gaultheria procumbens	Checkerberry
Lespedeza capitata	Bush Clover
Lespedeza simulata	Bush Clover
Mitchella repens	Partridge Berry
Pyrola chlorantha	Shin Leaf
Pyrola elliptica	Shin Leaf
Solidago bicolor	Golden-rod
Solidago canadensis	Golden-rod

FERNS

Aspidium marginale	Shield Fern
Aspidium spinulosum	Shield Fern
Lycopodium clavatum	Club Moss
Lycopodium complanatum	Club Moss
Lycopodium obscurum var. *dendroideum.*	Club Moss
Polystichum acrostichoides	Christmas Fern

CHAPTER VI

THE OAK WOODS

OAK woods are found on uplands. They rise above the streams and ponds, surround the sunny fields, fringe the juniper slopes, and cover many a hillside. Sometimes, on the one hand, there are aged white pines left among them on the ridges, and on the other hand the oaks themselves are left on the sides of ravines among beeches, maples and hemlocks.

There are many different kinds of oaks, white oaks and red oaks, scarlet, black and chestnut oaks. The white oaks and the red oaks grow side by side in about equal numbers and sometimes become great gnarled wide-branched trees. Because of their dominance, this woodland which is really composed of a rich variety of vegetation, is called the Oak Association.

In this woods, there are tulip trees, hickories and basswoods, which together with the oaks, make the highest growth. Below them are small trees and shrubs; dogwoods, hop hornbeams and sassafras, bladder nuts, witch-hazels and alternate-leaved dogwoods, pinxter flower, blue tangles, huckleberries and low sweet blueberries, New Jersey teas, arrow-woods and mountain laurels. In their midst honeysuckles, grapes, purple-flowering raspberries and *Clematis verticillaris* twine and tumble, and many herbaceous plants and ferns grow underneath. This makes a definitely layered formation which is distinctive of the oak association.

The sequence of its effects is also characteristic. At the very approach of spring the daintiest flowers find their way up through the fallen leaves; pastel-tinted hepaticas, rose-veined spring beauties and gray-rosetted saxifrages, snow-white arabis, tinted anemones and golden-stemmed gray-white blood-roots, anemonellas, heucheras, and bishop's caps. At the same time the oaks are opening their leaf buds in hazy grays, or in warm rose and copper tones. A little later the hickories unfold gray petal-like buds with reflexed scales glistening in gold, salmon and rose. And the ferns beneath are also uncurling their russet-scaled green fronds.

There are other flowers, too, tiny groundnuts, violet-fringed polygalas and all kinds of dainty violets. There are also wild gingers, solomon seals, yellow star grass and greenish yellow bellworts. There are wild geraniums, meadow rues, sarsaparillas, baneberries and false spikenard. Some of these are in bloom when the fleeting whiteness of dogwoods edge the woods, some accompany the clustered pink of *Rhododendron nudiflorum,* and some supplement the flowering of the mountain laurels; occasionally, arbutus is found.

At mid-summer, foxgloves and yellow loosestrifes, lavender and purple-flowered milkweeds, *Anemone virginiana* and *Cimicifuga racemosa,* the snake-root, rise here and there. Later still come the blue and white asters. They mingle their ethereal coloring with the richer autumn tones of the trees and shrubs. Bronze thickets of huckleberries are everywhere under the trees. Above them rise the lithe stems of the arrow-woods with clustered purplish black berries and rose-suffused leaves that have a marvelous mosaic translucence. Above there is the burnished rose, yellow, red and mahogany of the dogwoods, contrasting masses of red and yellow sassafras, the clear yellow of witch-hazels, the pale gold of tulip trees, the straw and russet brown of hickories, intermingled with the rich red and warm rose tones of the turning oaks. And here and there are scarlet dogwood berries that are but a glint and a gleam to be caught before the birds and squirrels make way with them.

Then in the winter the flaky silver-gray of the white oak trunks, the russet-touched huckleberry twigs, the green blueberry stems, and the bark browns and grays of the other trees and shrubs are all held together by the soft burnished browns of the dried oak leaves that stay on some of the oaks and form the ground cover of the woods. Then, the bared trees and shrubs exhibit the structural beauty of their trunks and branches, twigs and buds as at no other time. The stiff angular branching of the oaks, the lacy twiggage of the hop hornbeams, the loosened slabs of the shagbark hickories, the arching witch-hazel stems, the scalloped seed vessels of the tulip trees, the horizontal dogwood branches with their gracefully curved-up tips terminated by round turban-like buds, are all beautiful in their line drawing while the patterns made by the intermingled vegetation are veritable etchings.

These oak woodlands are found near the shore line of the Atlantic coast, all through the rolling country of Massachusetts, Connecticut, New York, Long Island, New Jersey and Pennsylvania, and upon the high ridges of the Alleghanies from Vermont to Georgia.

These are the woods, then, that are found on many a country estate. They provide the setting for the house and the background for the lawns and gardens. Their naturalistic character has an intrinsic beauty that pervades the entire property and that can be retained and reproduced in every part of it. A wide-branched tree often suggests a natural entrance and from it the drive can wind its way in gentle curves up to the house. With careful planning every tree of value can be retained and as little of the undergrowth as possible need be sacrificed for the road-bed. On either side of it the larger trees show their dark columns, the smaller trees make filmy screens, the herbaceous plants intermingle as ground covers and here and there, where there is sufficient light, shrubs appear ever so delicately. This planting is distinctive and is doubly significant when it is consistently brought up to the immediate surroundings of the house, used to encircle the terrace, forecourt and courtyard, and placed up against its very walls.

Pinxter flowers and blueberries, for instance, can be planted under the windows. Slender bladder nuts are good against narrow wall spaces. Alternate-leaved dogwoods and witch-hazels are effective at corners. *Clematis verticillaris* with pinkish purple flowers can be trained against the wall beside large-leaved fragrant wild grapes. And dogwoods, even hop hornbeams and sassafras, can be used everywhere, as wall screens, as courtyard enclosures, as accents for window groups and doors.

More than this, the woodland should imbue the house with its very spirit. It should suggest the building materials that are harmonious with it, such as weathered shingles, blackish slate, dark oak, soft-toned stucco, hand-made brick or stone. It should govern, too, the form of the house so that it with its ells and wings and surrounding buildings adapts itself to the natural contours of the land and to the character of the scene.

When the house is used only in the summer, it is often hidden deep in the woods. For all year around, however, it needs to be placed on the edge of a clearing in sunlight. Such an open space is found in the outlying fields and meadows that are frequent in the midst of old woodlots. Here lawns can be the terraces immediately about the house, while the rest of the grass can be left unclipped in keeping with the naturalistic surroundings. Here each great old tree, too, can be left as a wonderful feature.

It is important to keep or to recreate the spontaneous outlines of the woods. Along the edge, the natural decorativeness of trunks and branches, of twiggage, of varying foliage greens and of different leaf forms can be noticed. And there, the sunlight makes all the trees and shrubs flower abundantly.

The bloom of the dogwood is striking. These trees are often distributed so thickly that, at flower time at least, they seem to be the most significant. They constitute, however, only the first display. Here, *Rhododendron nudiflorum* is full of color. The mountain laurels, too, flower luxuriantly. The arrow-woods make a white flower line with flat panicles held on stems of equal height, and the New Jersey tea blossoms that come a little later are soft against the mid-summer green. In the meanwhile, the bladder nuts are delicately beautiful with drooping white flowers and the hop hornbeams have dangling spring-time fruit that is as green as their filmy birch-like leaves. Both of these trees can be used in small groups here and there to lighten the effect. About the same time the branches of the tulip trees, far overhead, hold out great flowers with reflexed green sepals and greenish-yellow petals painted with orange. Tulip trees generally grow singly and widely scattered. The tree is very striking because of the way its great columnar shaft rises straight up through the interwoven branches of other trees.

Another effect is always a surprise when toward the end of October the witch-hazels come unexpectedly into flower. They can be used in telling groups, for their light-filled yellow flowers add indescribable loveliness to the intermingled trees and shrubs.

Around these clearings lie the main woods. Bridle-paths and trails can be cut through to reach every part. First a wide path can be made all around the edges of the estate to outline the property's full extent and serve as fire barrier. Other paths may lead along the ridges, skirt a pasture or small clearing, dip down into the valley, cross a little stream by ford or stone bridge, climb a slope, pass rocky outcrops, mount the natural steps of ledges and reach the top of the hill for the view.

Sometimes, on a wood lot of perhaps fifty acres, it can take an hour or more to walk around the entire woods, but there are always cross paths, too, that make it possible to return in shorter time without retracing any steps. Such walks are always full of adventure, especially if there is an intimate knowledge of the woods.

It requires no little art to leave the woods absolutely natural and seemingly untouched. And yet, nature can be aided. Dried underbrush and dead trunks can be cleared away, crowded woods can be thinned, great old specimens can be singled out, and diseased and dying trees can be treated. Moreover, burnt-over areas can be encouraged. Even in the short period of five years a marked change will be noticed. The vigor of the older trees that have been saved from too severe fire will seem fully renewed. The sprouts that start from stumps will be approximately eighteen feet high. New branches will overarch the paths and shadows will begin to creep across them. The undergrowth, by that time, will be full grown again and the whole area will take on again the semblance of a real wood.

All during this time, new trees, new shrubs and new flowers can be planted. There are opportunities for the most delightful naturalizing. All the little plants that are so characteristic a part of the oak woods can be reëstablished. They can be assembled along the paths. Hepaticas, spring beauties, anemones, violets and bloodroots can be planted by the hundreds, even by the thousands in colonies. The maianthemum can be reëstablished in groups at the base of tree trunks. The groundnuts can be planted in little mats. Both have the tiniest slender-stalked flowers in spring. Close by them *Aster macrophyllus* with its large leaves can be planted in thick masses. The various depths of soil and the different degrees of light penetrating through the foliage overhead influence their special preferences as to sites. Some, like the wood betony, the milkweeds, the loosestrifes, as well as the arbutus (if it will grow at all), seek the sunny spots. Wild sarsaparillas, baneberries and bellworts gather in little clumps in the shade. Arabis and wild ginger, saxifrages and showy orchids, summer-flowering anemones and snakeroots are found in the natural rockeries. And amid all these are many kinds of graceful asters. There are, too, many kinds of ferns, the various botrychiums, *Aspidium marginale, Aspidium spinulosum, Woodsia obtusa* and, wherever limestone outcrops appear, is *Camptosorus rhizophyllus* or walking leaf.

These intermingled herbaceous plants make flower pictures that can be brought to their finest perfection where the paths draw near the house. The garden below the terrace, beside the porch, or within the courtyard can be kept in the spirit of this planting, with the choicest of the trees, shrubs and flowers reserved for it. Tall tulip trees may rise above it or a great oak may shelter it. Dogwoods can be planted all around it and may also be used as specimens within the garden. Masses of mountain laurel in irregular hedgings will in a comparatively few years become shoulder-high.

Within such an enclosure the borders can be edged with *Mitella diphylla*, the bishop's cap, *Heuchera americana*, the alum root, and *Tiarella cordifolia*, the false mitre-wort. In spring their delicate white spires fill the garden, with the white of dogwoods above them. A little later they make a green cover with rosettes of lobed and heart-shaped leaves. Violets can be planted everywhere among them: *Viola pubescens*, the downy yellow violets, *Viola latiuscula*, *Viola palmata*, *Viola triloba*, and *Viola rostrata*, the long-spurred violets all found growing under oaks.

All these plants can be used, too, as a kind of groundwork for groups of light green ferns, white lacy-foliaged meadow-rues, decorative solomon seals, false spikenard, dainty gerardias, and the most delicate of the wood asters. Squaw huckleberries may be planted among them, far apart in the manner that they naturally grow. These are precious shrubs with loosely arranged horizontal sprays, soft foliage, and the most delightful little bell-shaped white blossoms with decorative russet-toned stamens.

This would make a green and white garden with violets, light blue asters and blush and pink mountain laurels to offset it. It would be a garden where leaf

[51]

forms and foliage textures would count as much as the flowers. It would be a garden of infinite refinement, an enviable garden to have close to the house.

The owner of the large estate has begun to understand the rich heritage that is his. He is appreciating the landscape value of the oak woods, is preserving their beauty and allowing their character to control the character of his house and its surroundings. The owner of a few acres has the same opportunities even if he has not quite so varied a landscape. He, too, can retain the roadside growth, build his house under the trees, reëstablish the natural outlines of the clearing and preserve the real charm of the woods in their minutest details.

Many suburban communities are becoming established upon the wooded ridges that surround our cities. It is to be hoped that the natural beauty of these places will be fully realized before the untutored ax clears it away in preparing house sites as it has too often done before. Many suburban dwellers prefer roads that hold the charm of country lanes, with houses nestled cosily beneath great trees and surrounded with the growth that belongs there. Too many opportunities for beauty have been lost in sacrificing all the undergrowth and thinning the woods.

Isolated forest trees soon become diseased and die. And yet, wherever a few trees still remain, wherever a solitary hickory, a group of oaks or a few scattered tulip trees are left to give a clue, they can become the nucleus around which the vegetation that belongs to the oak woods may again be planted. Even on small

The Oak Woods

lots with but a single big tree, the characteristic small trees and shrubs can be planted against the house and around the lawns, and the natural flowers and ferns can be gathered together in pleasant sun-flecked gardens.

THE OAK ASSOCIATION

TREES

Carya alba	Mocker Nut
Carya glabra	Pignut
Carya ovata	Shag-bark Hickory
Cornus florida	Flowering Dogwood
Liriodendron Tulipifera	Tulip Tree
Morus alba *	White Mulberry
Ostrya virginiana	Hop Hornbeam
Prunus pennsylvanica	Wild Red Cherry
Prunus serotina	Wild Black Cherry
Pyrus americana	American Mountain Ash
Quercus alba	White Oak
Quercus coccinea	Scarlet Oak
Quercus Muhlenbergii	Yellow Oak
Quercus Prinus	Chestnut Oak
Quercus rubra	Red Oak
Quercus stellata	Post Oak
Quercus velutina	Black Oak
Sassafras variifolium	Sassafras
Tilia americana	Basswood

SHRUBS AND VINES

Amelanchier canadensis	Shad Bush
Ceanothus americanus	New Jersey Tea
Celastrus scandens	Bitter-sweet
Clematis verticillaris	Clematis
Cornus alternifolia	Alternate-leaved Dogwood
Diervilla Lonicera	Bush Honeysuckle
Gaylussacia frondosa	Blue Tangle
Hamamelis virginiana	Witch-hazel
Ilex verticillata	Winterberry
Kalmia latifolia	Mountain Laurel
Lonicera sempervirens	Trumpet Honeysuckle
Rhamnus cathartica *	Common Buckthorn
Rhododendron nudiflorum	Pinxter Flower
Ribes Cynosbati	Prickly Gooseberry
Ribes rotundifolium	Gooseberry
Rosa setigera	Climbing Rose

[53]

American Plants for American Gardens

SHRUBS AND VINES (Continued)

Rubus odoratus ....Purple-flowering Raspberry
Staphylea trifolia ....Bladder Nut
Vaccinium pennsylvanicum ....Low Sweet Blueberry
Vaccinium stamineum ....Squaw Huckleberry
Vaccinium vacillans ....Late Low Blueberry
Viburnum acerifolium ....Arrow-wood
Vitis æstivalis ....Summer Grape
Vitis labrusca ....Northern Fox Grape

HERBS

Actea alba ....White Baneberry
Actea rubra ....Red Baneberry
Anaphalis margaritacea ....Pearly Everlasting
Anemone quinquefolia ....Wood Anemone
Anemone virginiana ....Anemone
Anemonella thalictroides ....Rue Anemone
Antennaria neglecta ....Everlasting
Antennaria neodioica ....Everlasting
Antennaria plantaginifolia ....Plantain-leaved Everlasting
Aquilegia canadensis ....Wild Columbine
Arabis lyrata ....Rock Cress
Aralia nudicaulis ....Wild Sarsaparilla
Asarum canadense ....Wild Ginger
Asclepias phytolaccoides ....Poke Milkweed
Asclepias quadrifolia ....Milkweed
Asclepias variegata ....Milkweed
Aster acuminatus ....Aster
Aster cordifolius ....Aster
Aster divaricatus ....Aster
Aster infirmus ....Aster
Aster linariifolius ....Aster
Aster macrophyllus ....Aster
Aster prenanthoides ....Aster
Baptisia tinctoria ....Wild Indigo
Chimaphila maculata ....Spotted Wintergreen
Chimaphila umbellata ....Pipsissewa
Cimicifuga racemosa ....Black Snakeroot
Claytonia virginica ....Spring Beauty
Comandra umbellata ....Bastard Toad-flax
Corydalis sempervirens ....Pale Corydalis
Cynoglossum virginianum ....Wild Comfrey
Cypripedium acaule ....Lady's Slipper
Epigaea repens ....Mayflower
Galium Aparine ....Cleavers
Galium circaezans ....Wild Liquorice
Galium lanceolatum ....Wild Liquorice
Gaultheria procumbens ....Checkerberry

[54]

The Oak Woods

HERBS (Continued)

Geranium maculatum .... Wild Cranesbill
Gerardia flava .... Downy False Foxglove
Gerardia virginica .... Smooth False Foxglove
Hepatica triloba .... Hepatica
Heuchera americana .... Common Alum Root
Hieracium venosum .... Poor Robin's Plantain
Hypoxis hirsuta .... Star Grass
Lespedeza capitata .... Bush Clover
Lespedeza simulata .... Bush Clover
Luzula parviflora .... Wood Rush
Lysimachia quadrifolia .... Loosestrife
Maianthemum canadense .... Maianthemum
Melampyrum lineare .... Cow Wheat
Mitchella repens .... Partridge Berry
Mitella diphylla .... Bishop's Cap
Oakesia sessilifolia .... Oakesia
Orchis spectabilis .... Showy Orchis
Oxalis filipes .... Wood Sorrel
Oxalis violacea .... Violet Wood Sorrel
Panax trifolium .... Groundnut
Pedicularis canadensis .... Wood Betony
Pentstemon lævigatus var. Digitalis...... Beard-tongue
Polygala pauciflora .... Fringed Polygala
Polygonatum biflorum .... Small Solomon's Seal
Potentilla canadensis .... Cinquefoil
Potentilla pumila .... Cinquefoil
Prunella vulgaris .... Self-heal
Pyrola chlorantha .... Shin Leaf
Pyrola elliptica .... Shin Leaf
Sanguinaria canadensis .... Bloodroot
Saxifraga virginiensis .... Early Saxifrage
Scrophularia leporella .... Figwort
Smilacena racemosa .... False Spikenard
Solidago bicolor .... Golden-rod
Solidago cæsia .... Golden-rod
Solidago latifolia .... Golden-rod
Solidago squarrosa .... Golden-rod
Thalictrum dioicum .... Early Meadow Rue
Thalictrum revolutum .... Meadow Rue
Tiarella cordifolia .... False Miterwort
Triosteum auranticum .... Horse Gentian
Uvularia grandiflora .... Bellwort
Uvularia perfoliata .... Bellwort
Veronica officinalis .... Speedwell
Viola latiuscula .... Violet
Viola palmata .... Violet
Viola pubescens .... Downy Yellow Violet

American Plants for American Gardens

HERBS (Continued)

Viola rostrata ....Long-spurred Violet
Viola triloba ....Violet

FERNS

Aspidium marginale ....Shield Fern
Aspidium noveboracense ....Shield Fern
Aspidium spinulosum ....Shield Fern
Asplenium platyneuron ....Spleenwort
Asplenium Ruta-muraria ....Spleenwort
Asplenium Trichomanes ....Spleenwort
Botrychium obliquum var. *dissectum* ....Moonwort
Botrychium simplex ....Moonwort
Botrychium ternatum ....Moonwort
Botrychium virginianum ....Rattlesnake Fern
Camptosorus rhizophyllus ....Walking Leaf
Lycopodium clavatum ....Club Moss
Lycopodium lucidulum ....Club Moss
Lycopodium obscurum var. *dendroideum*.Club Moss
Pellæa atropurpurea ....Cliff Brake
Polypodium vulgare ....Polypody
Polystichum acrostichoides ....Christmas Fern
Polystichum acrostichoides var. *Schwein-
itzii* ....Christmas Fern
Pteris aquilina ....Brake
Woodsia obtusa ....Woodsia

CHAPTER VII

THE BEECH-MAPLE-HEMLOCK WOODS

BEECHES, maples and hemlocks are found growing together in old and stately woods. The hemlocks are tall evergreen trees with seal brown trunks, drooping branches and short flat needles. The maples are sturdy round-topped trees. Their trunks are furrowed and gray-brown, their strong branches are noticeably upright, their leaves are deeply lobed. The beeches are broad symmetrical trees. Their smooth trunks are steel gray, their horizontal branches are placed in widespread tiers, their slender buds and pointed leaves are arranged far apart on spray-like stems.

These three trees occur in varied proportions according to the quality of the soil, the amount of moisture and the temperature. Sometimes, there are almost all hemlocks, as in the far north and on high mountains. These forests are dark and green. Then again, there are almost all maples, as in the far south, whose open branching allows the light to filter through thickly clustered foliage. And sometimes, in places where the climate is moderate and the soil is very rich, there are all beeches. These woods are marked by the grayness of their trunks and twigs. When all three trees are about equally able to adapt themselves to prevailing conditions they intermingle and form a mixed woods that is known as the Beech-Maple-Hemlock Association.

The charm of this association depends upon the way the three trees appear together in all stages of their growth. There are century-old specimens of gigantic size and incomparable beauty and saplings that have all the loveliness of bark and trunk, of branch and twig, of leaf and bud that is so delightful in maturer trees. This intermingling of trees of all ages is a characteristic unique to the Beech-Maple-Hemlock Association.

The young trees take the place of the undergrowth usual in other woods, but occasionally a few other trees and shrubs are mingled with them. There may be scattered groups of white birches, black birches and yellow birches, masses of mountain laurels, ground covers of evergreen yews. There may be arrow-wood, striped maples and mountain maples appearing here and there and, also, occasional dogwoods, witch-hazels and alternate-leaved dogwoods.

The interlacing branches make the woods quite shady. Herbaceous plants are, therefore, only found where sufficient light can penetrate. Then there are violets and trilliums, dutchman's breeches and spikenards, bellworts and star-flowers, wild ginger, twisted stalks and Indian cucumber-roots, and various other little plants with delightfully delicate flowers, foliage and fruit. Ferns take their place wherever there is deeper shade, and waxy Indian pipes and brown beech

drops are found in the darkest spots. All these other
trees, shrubs, flowers and ferns are only incidental to
the three main trees and it is this incidental quality
that forms a foil for the dignity of the beeches, maples
and hemlocks.

These woods exist only in remote places and are
on land that has been untouched for a long time.
Many of them have been cut for lumber or to make
way for farming and grazing lands. Whenever they
are destroyed they seem utterly lost, for it takes over a
century to replace them. Only a very few of the age-
old forests remain and they are veritable landmarks.
Even the younger woods are becoming comparatively
rare. Their beauty is so precious that every effort
to preserve them is worth-while. Their preservation
makes a special appeal to every lover of trees.

Such a woods makes a priceless estate and an impressive setting for a great house. The first problem
in connection with it is always the plotting of the
drive. And this is more than a question of engineering, for, in arranging lines and curves, the spirit of
the woods has to be retained with the finest parts of
the young growth preserved and every great tree effectively singled out. The opening of the drive gives
a chance for observing not only the loveliest stretches
of beeches, maples and hemlocks but the incidental
growth. Groups of birches will grow along the sides.
The colorful glossy trunks of the white birches, of the
black birches and of the yellow birches can be made
enlivening notes among the other trees. All of these
birches are slender trees with arching branches and

showery clusters of thin twigs from which the finely serrated leaves hang in filmy effect. At mid-summer the birch foliage is light and airy and in the autumn it is touched with yellow, the olive-yellow tone of the yellow birches being particularly lovely. There are, also, the striped maples, their trunks marked with green and yellow-white. In the fall their large leaves turn straw-colored. There are mountain maples, too, that are shrub-like with noticeable large leaves that are conspicuously orange and red in the autumn. Here and there the wayfaring trees can be distinguished by the rigorous structure of their horizontal branches. Their large white flowers are an outstanding feature of the spring while the wine-red tone of their foliage adds a rich note to the woods in the fall. There are, too, yews and mountain laurels and occasional dogwoods and witch-hazels. All these trees and shrubs will grow luxuriantly wherever the building of the drive admits sunlight. In back of them, there will be the deep, undisturbed, even shade that is so distinctly characteristic of the beech-maple-hemlock woods.

The drive can be continued to a point where a view suggests a site for the house. Where there is no natural clearing the woods has to be opened up to provide sufficient sunlight. They should be thinned with the greatest care and every effective tree left to become a feature of the lawn. Where they have plenty of space maples become beautifully symmetrical and beeches become wide-spread and statuesque. Besides, circles of young beeches have a way of developing around great old beeches. These are so full of interest that they are worth keeping.

The house itself can become a part of its setting when the plan, the height of the walls, the pitch of the roof and the length of the chimneys can be adapted to the contours and when the material of the house can be in keeping with the dignity of the woods. This will be evident even at a distance when a glimpse of the house is caught in the midst of the trees. In a nearer view the link between the house and its setting can be made stronger through the planting, by the use of laurels and yews, of wayfaring trees and birches, of striped maples and mountain maples planted against the walls. And beeches and hemlocks can be planted as hedges for the courtyards and gardens. All these trees and shrubs ought to be planted about the entire area immediately around the house and lawn so that they can blend imperceptibly into the woodland.

Grounds of more limited area are also full of opportunities. Even the small place, in the shelter of a hillside still covered with beeches, maples and hemlocks can use a planting plan composed entirely of the trees and shrubs, flowers and ferns that belong there. Just a single great tree left standing upon a property can suggest a similar planting. There striped and mountain maples, hemlocks and beeches can be arranged in unclipped hedges and hedgerows. Then yellow birches can be chosen to mark the entrance, specimen yews can be planted on either side of the doorway, ferns and laurels can make borders below the windows and groups of wayfaring trees or birches can be planted at the corners.

The outstretched branches of the great tree can shelter a tiny terrace. This terrace may be paved and then bordered with yews and ferns and edged with violets, tiarellas and heucheras. This tree can also cast its shade upon a little garden with paths and steps that wind between irregular borders adapted to the slope and with planting that accentuates the naturalistic character of the grounds. There white birches may be used as accents and the lithe-stemmed maple-leaved viburnums can be used in scattered clumps amid a profusion of flowers and ferns. Masses of dutchman's breeches can be planted in the rocky outcrops among little spleenworts, polypods, purple cliff brakes and beech ferns. Wild ginger with satiny heart-shaped leaves may grow in clumps nearby. Trilliums can be gathered at the base of the tree trunks. The painted trilliums, *Trillium undulatum,* and the large white-flowered *Trillium grandiflora* with heavy ovate leaves, the nodding trilliums, *Trillium cernuum,* whose fragrant flowers hide beneath the foliage, and *Trillium erectum,* with a comparatively long stalk that holds a single terminal purple-red flower above the usual whorl of three leaves can be used. These are offset by the great fronds of marginal shield ferns. There are, too, baneberries and false solomon seals to gather into clumps among the maple-leaved viburnums. Some of the taller ferns like *Aspidium spinulosum* can be intermingled with them. Heucheras, tiarellas and bishop's caps can be

The Beech-Maple-Hemlock Woods

planted along the paths and can show their little white
spires and rosetted leaves in between groups of Christmas ferns. Besides, all sorts of delicately modeled
flowers like the drooping bellworts, the nodding green
solomon seals, the twisted stalks, the seven-petaled
star-flowers and Indian cucumber-roots can be arranged in scattered groups here and there. And
violets can be planted as a ground cover for all the
other flowers. There is the tiny white violet, *Viola
blanda,* that is faintly sweet-scented. There is the
blue and white *Viola palmata* with cut leaves. There
is the downy yellow violet, *Viola pubescens,* the long
spurred violet, *Viola rostrata,* and the woolly blue
violet, *Viola sororia,* whose flowers grade from lavender to violet and are held above the leaves.

These intimate little flowers make delightfully informal gardens but their real value lies in the way
they complete the setting suggested by the existing
great tree and help to create the atmosphere of a natural beech-maple-hemlock association.

THE BEECH-MAPLE-HEMLOCK ASSOCIATION

TREES

Acer pennsylvanicum	Striped Maple
Acer saccharum	Sugar Maple
Acer spicatum	Mountain Maple
Betula alba	White Birch
Betula lenta	Black Birch
Betula lutea	Yellow Birch
Castanea dentata	Chestnut
Cornus florida	Flowering Dogwood
Fagus grandifolia	Beech
Fraxinus americana	White Ash
Liriodendron Tulipifera	Tulip Tree
Tilia americana	Basswood
Tsuga canadensis	Hemlock

[63]

American Plants for American Gardens

SHRUBS

Amelanchier canadensis ....Shad Bush
Amelanchier oblongifolia ....Juneberry
Cornus alternifolia ....Alternate-leaved Dogwood
Hamamelis virginiana ....Witch-hazel
Kalmia latifolia ....Mountain Laurel
Taxus canadensis ....American Yew
Viburnum acerifolium ....Arrow-wood
Viburnum Lantana ....Wayfaring Tree

HERBS

Actæa alba ....White Baneberry
Actæa rubra ....Red Baneberry
Asarum canadense ....Wild Ginger
Circæa lutetiana ....Enchanter's Nightshade
Cornus canadensis ....Bunchberry
Cypripedium acaule ....Stemless Lady's Slipper
Dicentra Cucullaria ....Dutchman's Breeches
Epifagus virginiana ....Beech-drops
Eupatorium urticæfolium ....White Snakeroot
Geranium Robertianum ....Herb Robert
Heuchera americana ....Common Alum Root
Luzula parviflora ....Wood Rush
Maianthemum canadense ....Maianthemum
Medeola virginiana ....Indian Cucumber-root
Mitchella repens ....Partridge Berry
Mitella diphylla ....Bishop's Cap
Monotropa uniflora ....Indian Pipe
Orchis spectabilis ....Showy Orchis
Oxalis Acetosella ....Common Wood Sorrel
Oxalis violacea ....Violet Wood Sorrel
Polygonatum biflorum ....Small Solomon's Seal
Prenanthes alba ....White Lettuce
Prenanthes trifoliolata ....Gall-of-the-earth
Smilacina racemosa ....False Spikenard
Streptopus roseus ....Twisted-stalk
Tiarella cordifolia ....False Miterwort
Trientalis americana ....Star Flower
Trillium erectum ....Wake Robin
Trillium grandiflorum ....Wake Robin
Uvularia grandiflora ....Bellwort
Uvularia perfoliata ....Bellwort
Viola blanda ....Violet
Viola palmata ....Violet
Viola pubescens ....Downy Yellow Violet
Viola rostrata ....Long-spurred Violet
Viola sororia ....Violet
Viola triloba ....Violet

[64]

The Beech-Maple-Hemlock Woods

Ferns

Adiantum pedatum .... Maidenhair
Aspidium marginale .... Shield Fern
Aspidium noveboracense .... Shield Fern
Aspidium spinulosum .... Shield Fern
Asplenium Filix-femina .... Lady Fern
Asplenium platyneuron .... Spleenwort
Asplenium Ruta-muraria .... Spleenwort
Asplenium Trichomanes .... Spleenwort
Botrychium obliquum var. *dissectum* ...Moonwort
Botrychium ternatum .... Moonwort
Botrychium virginianum .... Rattlesnake Fern
Camptosorus rhizophyllus .... Walking Leaf
Cystopteris fragilis .... Bladder Fern
Dicksonia punctilobula .... Hay-scented Fern
Pellæa atropurpurea .... Cliff Brake
Phegopteris Dryopteris .... Oak Fern
Phegopteris hexagonoptera .... Beech Fern
Phegopteris polypodioides .... Beech Fern
Polypodium vulgare .... Polypody
Polystichum acrostichoides .... Christmas Fern
Woodsia obtusa .... Woodsia

CHAPTER VIII

THE HEMLOCK RAVINE

HEMLOCKS grow on the side of deep ravines. Their roots find foothold between big boulders. Their tall dark trunks tower beside great cliffs. Their soft branches throw shadows over fern-covered rocks. In the deep hollows water trickles over mossy ledges. All is dark and cool and green. Even at noon-day when the sun is high the wood is held in lavender light.

In the rich moist ravines of the north, the ground is covered with yews. These low shrubs with their short-needled branches repeat the delicate structure of the hemlocks above them. Farther south, throughout the Alleghanies, rhododendrons grow in these deep woods. Their leaves are large and leathery, their green rich and glossy. They grow tree-like with wide-flung angular branches that often arch overhead. Mountain laurels with their luxuriant evergreen are found there, both in the north and in the south. So, too, is the *Viburnum alnifolium,* or hobble-bush. It has a vigorous structure, horizontal branches, large white flowers and generous heart-shaped leaves that are a rich wine-red in the fall. There are, also, striped maples and mountain maples. The striped maple is particularly noticeable for its trunk has vertical alternately green and yellow-white markings.

The Hemlock Ravine

Many delicate plants, too, grow in these woods: bishop's caps with dainty white spires, heucheras with their airy flowers, violets, golden saxifrages, bellworts, solomon's seals, bunchberries, wild gingers and many another whose foliage is as delightful as the flowers.

The flooring of the woods depends, however, for its real loveliness upon its many ferns. On the flat tops of the rocks are luxuriant mats of little polypods. On their vertical sides, caught in the niches, are cliff brakes and rock brakes. Frail bladder ferns seek foothold nearer the water and cling to wet boulders. Maidenhairs seek the moist ground nearby. Sometimes spleenworts grow there, too. These ferns are, however, less dependent upon moisture and are found as well on the sides of the ravine. Their slender little clusters often spring up beside cliff brakes and tuck themselves in among polypods. Their long glossy black stems make effective silhouettes against gray lichen-covered rocks. And, sometimes, among all these there are walking ferns. Their curious long-tapered leaves reach out, touch the rock, take root, form new plants and, thus reproducing themselves, trail further year by year across huge limestone ledges. Woodsias, too, grow in luxuriant masses. They are all silvery green in the spring-time. *Woodsia ilvensis* is often found within a few feet of the trickling water, while *Woodsia obtusa* loves the stony hillsides and grows either in the sun on the very top or on dry rocks in shady places. And luxuriant dark-toned evergreen Christmas ferns grow in satisfying masses wherever rich earth fills the spaces between rock and ledge. There are, besides, *Aspidium marginale* and *Aspidium spinulosum*. Both are tall evergreen ferns of graceful habit. They gather together in delightful groups. They assume the place of shrubs in situations that do not permit shrubs to grow. They are particularly fine where they have room really to express themselves. And in these woods, so rich in ferns, even the mosses have a fern-like character and spread their leaf-like patterns flat upon the rocks.

This scene, filled with varying tones of quiet green, lies in such subdued light and is held in such soft shadows that it seems caught in enchantment. This atmosphere is worth preserving even.if our grounds are small and there is but a single old hemlock upon them.

It may be that the house can be built right beside the tree, almost under its branches, and that the windows, porch or paved terrace can open upon a hemlock-shaded garden surrounded with laurels and rhododendron and matted with yews and ferns. The hemlock may, however, be in a more secluded spot away from the house, often on the side of the hill, guarding rocks and ledges with a stream nearby to trickle over the stones. This can be made into a delightfully cool retreat. If the hemlock happens to be situated in a less fortunate spot a few great rocks can be brought in to form a quiet nook and a rough stone seat can be built into a shady corner. A hidden pipe can be installed, too, so that water can drip slowly, intermittently even, over some of the stones. Such a place can be made into an ideal fern garden. The twenty or more different kinds found in hemlock ravines, and here described, can be gathered together and put into congenial situations such as they have in the woods. This is not just a miscellaneous collection. They naturally belong together and for that reason are really effective.

In creating such a natural scene, masses of the big *Aspidium marginale,* the shield fern, can be planted as a background. Colonies of little polypods, growing luxuriantly either in sun or shade, can be spread over the tops of the rocks. Wherever there are limestone rocks, mats of *Camptosorus rhizophyllus,* the walking leaf, can be established. Innumerable *Asplenium platyneuron,* one of the delicate spleenworts, *Pellea atropurpurea,* the cliff brake, and the rosetted *Woodsia obtusa* can be planted here and there in the crevices between the rocks. *Cryptogramma Stelleari,* the slender rock brake, can be used to fill every little soil pocket. Patches of the moss-like *Selaginella rupestris* and the soft silvery green *Woodsia ilvensis* are worth trying on dry exposed places. In shady spots, *Asplenium Ruta-muraria,* the little spleenwort, *Asplenium Trichomanes,* the tiny tufted spleenwort, *Phegopteris Dryopteris,* the spreading light green oak fern, and *Phegopteris hexagonoptera,* the beech fern with broad triangular fronds, may be placed in groups. Close to the rocks, to show against them, *Phegopteris polypodioides,* one of the beech ferns, *Aspidium spinulosum,* the wood fern, and *Aspidium*

[69]

noveboracense, another wood fern, can be planted in larger clumps. *Cystopteris bulbifera,* the bladder fern, with delicate trailing fronds, should be put right under the water's drip with *Cystopteris fragilis* near by. In the moist soil, where the water actually spreads over the ground, luxuriant groups of delicate maidenhairs can be established. In addition to all these, *Polystichum acrostichoides,* the Christmas fern, can be used everywhere, for they are luxuriantly green through the year like the hemlock that spreads its branches over them.

The real beauty of the hemlocks is felt most, of course, when they are in a real ravine. An estate is very fortunate when it encompasses such a scene, for such hemlock woods are rare. It is, therefore, a real privilege to preserve the scene wherever it has been left undisturbed and to bring it back if it has been neglected. A few of the great old trees must be there to make the picture real. Young hemlocks can, however, be brought in, for it is usual to find hemlocks of all ages together and the young trees have the same graciousness as the older ones. Then it is possible to plant again all the little ground covers and ferns, or at least to fill in the places where they have been destroyed. It is especially worth while to use the plants in their proper proportions, to place them in their true relationships to one another, and to arrange them in characteristic compositions in order to recreate the spirit of the original woods.

A great house can be splendidly placed at the top of such a ravine and built so that it will seem to be towering above the hemlock branches into the sunlight. Cliff-like walls, steep-hipped roofs and tall chimneys are appropriate and all the plants of the ravine can be placed immediately about the house. Yews and laurels, beautifully evergreen, *Viburnum alnifolium* with striking silhouettes, striped and mountain maples with effective foliage and stemmage can be used against the walls. A series of terraces can mold the house to its steep slope, paved with rough stone, offset by hedges of yews and supported by great retaining walls. Steps can adapt themselves to the rocks and ledges. They can be edged with heucheras, bellworts, bunchberries, and maianthemum, and all the little soil pockets between the stones can be filled with ferns. These steps can give way to moss-covered paths that wander between the rocks, along the stream, among the boulders and through every part of the green, fern-spread woods.

THE RAVINE ASSOCIATION

TREES

Acer pennsylvanicum	Striped Maple
Acer saccharum	Sugar Maple
Acer spicatum	Mountain Maple
Betula alba	White Birch
Betula lenta	Black Birch
Betula lutea	Yellow Birch
Carpinus caroliniana	Ironwood
Carya cordiformis	Bitter Nut
Cornus florida	Flowering Dogwood
Fagus grandifolia	Beech
Fraxinus americana	White Ash
Juglans cinerea	Butternut
Liriodendron Tulipifera	Tulip Tree
Salix babylonica	Weeping Willow
Salix nigra	Black Willow
Thuja occidentalis	Arbor Vitæ

American Plants for American Gardens

Trees (Continued)

Tilia americana .... Basswood
Tsuga canadensis .... Hemlock

Shrubs

Alnus incana .... Hoary Alder
Alnus rugosa .... Smooth Alder
Amelanchier canadensis .... Shad Bush
Hamamelis virginiana .... Witch-hazel
Kalmia latifolia .... Mountain Laurel
Lonicera canadensis .... American Fly Honeysuckle
Rhododendron maximum .... Great Laurel
Salix cordata .... Willow
Salix discolor .... Glaucous Willow
Salix glaucophylla .... Willow
Salix lucida .... Shining Willow
Taxus canadensis .... American Yew
Viburnum alnifolium .... Hobble-bush

Herbs

Actæa alba .... White Baneberry
Actæa rubra .... Red Baneberry
Aquilegia canadensis .... Wild Columbine
Arabis lyrata .... Rock Cress
Arisæma Dracontium .... Green Dragon
Arisæma triphyllum .... Jack-in-the-Pulpit
Asarum canadense .... Wild Ginger
Asclepias incarnata .... Swamp Milkweed
Campanula rotundifolia .... Bluebell
Chrysosplenium americanum .... Golden Saxifrage
Cornus canadensis .... Bunchberry
Corydalis sempervirens .... Pale Corydalis
Cypripedium acaule .... Stemless Lady's Slipper
Dicentra Cucullaria .... Dutchman's Breeches
Epifagus virginiana .... Beech-drops
Erythronium americanum .... Yellow Adder's Tongue
Eupatorium perfoliatum .... Boneset
Eupatorium purpureum .... Joe Pye Weed
Heuchera americana .... Common Alum Root
Maianthemum canadense .... Maianthemum
Medeola virginiana .... Indian Cucumber-root
Mitchella repens .... Partridge Berry
Mitella diphylla .... Bishop's Cap
Oxalis Acetosella .... Common Wood Sorrel
Oxalis violacea .... Violet Wood Sorrel
Parnassia caroliniana .... Grass of Parnassus
Pilea pumila .... Clearweed

[72]

The Hemlock Ravine

HERBS (Continued)

Polygonatum biflorum .... Small Solomon's Seal
Potentilla argentea .... Silvery Cinquefoil
Potentilla tridentata .... Three-toothed Cinquefoil
Prenanthes alba .... White Lettuce
Sagina nodosa .... Pearlwort
Sanguisorba minor * .... Garden Burnet
Saxifraga virginiensis .... Early Saxifrage
Sedum acre * .... Mossy Stonecrop
Smilacina racemosa .... False Spikenard
Streptopus roseus .... Twisted-stalk
Thalictrum dioicum .... Early Meadow Rue
Thalictrum revolutum .... Meadow Rue
Trientalis americana .... Star Flower
Trillium declinatum .... Wake Robin
Trillium erectum .... Wake Robin
Trillium grandiflorum .... Wake Robin
Trillium undulatum .... Painted Trillium
Uvularia grandiflora .... Bellwort
Uvularia perfoliata .... Bellwort
Viola blanda .... Violet
Viola palmata .... Violet
Viola rostrata .... Long-spurred Violet
Viola rotundifolia .... Early Yellow Violet

FERNS

Adiantum pedatum .... Maidenhair
Aspidium marginale .... Shield Fern
Aspidium marginale var. elegans .... Shield Fern
Aspidium noveboracense .... Shield Fern
Aspidium spinulosum .... Shield Fern
Asplenium acrostichoides .... Spleenwort
Asplenium platyneuron .... Spleenwort
Asplenium Ruta-muraria .... Spleenwort
Asplenium Trichomanes .... Spleenwort
Botrychium virginianum .... Rattlesnake Fern
Camptosorus rhizophyllus .... Walking Leaf
Cryptogramma Stelleri .... Rock Brake
Cystopteris bulbifera .... Bladder Fern
Cystopteris fragilis .... Bladder Fern
Equisetum pratense .... Horsetail
Onoclea sensibilis .... Sensitive Fern
Pellæa atropurpurea .... Cliff Brake
Phegopteris Dryopteris .... Oak Fern
Phegopteris hexagonoptera .... Beech Fern
Phegopteris polypodioides .... Beech Fern
Polypodium vulgare .... Polypody

[73]

FERNS (*Continued*)

Polystichum acrostichoides . . . . Christmas Fern
Polystichum acrostichoides var. *Schwein-
itzii* . . . . Christmas Fern
Selaginella rupestris . . . . Selaginella
Woodsia ilvensis . . . . Woodsia
Woodsia obtusa . . . . Woodsia

CHAPTER IX

THE STREAM-SIDE

Many kinds of trees, a great variety of shrubs and innumerable herbaceous plants grow along streams and rivers. The ever-present supply of water and the moisture-laden atmosphere give them an ideal environment. And, as the stream meanders between low margins, under high banks, below gentle slopes and through flat low-lying areas, the varying amounts of water in the soil influence the selection and arrangement of the vegetation.

Elms sometimes define the course of the stream and grow on the well-drained slopes on either side. They are found as single specimens with tall graceful shapes, and as thickets where they are tangled and netted with wild grapes. Sycamores grow singly along the water-side and attract attention by their bark. Willows arrange themselves in almost regular rows along the margins, especially where the water is placid and slow moving. There are many different kinds of native willows, but they are very much alike and seem like gigantic shrubs with many crooked branches rising out of a short, stout trunk. The weeping willow with its long streamers is a European variety that has become naturalized in some places and is quite different from our native kinds.

Other trees gather together beside the water and cover the flat-lands as a mixed woods. There are balsam poplars and box elders, silver maples and ashes, mulberries and hawthorns, hackberries and sweet gums, bitter nuts and hickories. Here and there basswoods attract attention when their flowers send forth their fragrance, Canada plums become noticeable when their trees are covered with white bloom and occasional walnuts stand out as magnificent specimens. It is the luxuriance and greenness of the foliage, however, that is the special beauty of these intermingled trees. This is characteristic of much of the vegetation that is adapted to an abundant water supply.

Among the shrubs there are low bushy sweet gales, sweet pepper bushes with fragrant summer flowers, kinnikinniks and red-osier dogwoods, ninebarks and arrow-woods. There are clumps of elders and of witch-hazels, occasional bladder nuts, rows of spicebushes and groups of *Viburnum Lentago*. Alders, ironwoods and hop hornbeams grow in little inlets, shad bushes like the glens, while pin oaks, bur oaks and swamp white oaks or red maples and black alders thrive in low, wet places. The pin oaks and swamp white oaks draw attention by the drooping sweep of their lower branches. These two trees are otherwise quite different, for the pin oak has a straight, shaft-like trunk and the swamp white oak has a divided top, ending in many twisted branches. The red maples are the most conspicuous of all. Their spring twigs, swelling buds and opening blossoms are all a

brilliant red, their summer fruit crimson, and their
autumn foliage scarlet, while in the winter the effectiveness of their light gray trunks is heightened by
the scarlet berries and black-brown branches of the
black alders, *Ilex verticilata,* that grow among
them.

All this varied vegetation, together with myriad
herbaceous plants and ferns is found everywhere in
our Northeastern States, for the countryside has
many streams of every size. One stream with, perhaps, a tributary or two may be found upon almost
every large estate. Sometimes, to be sure, it is but
a minor note in the landscape and must be sought
out in the low meadow. But in many places it lends
such a charm to the property that attention can well
be focused upon it. The house can be placed within
view of the water. The lawns can slope down to
the edges. Paths may lead along the margins. The
entire estate with entrance drive and court, terrace
and garden can be adapted to it. And the vegetation
characteristic to stream-sides can be preserved or
recreated.

This is not so difficult to do. The natural growth
of plants in such favorable situations is comparatively rapid. The fibrous roots make it possible to
transplant large-sized material. And almost all this
vegetation adapts itself to somewhat drier ground
as well and can be planted therefore in the well-
drained places that will undoubtedly be selected for
the location of the house.

At the entrance of such a stream-side estate are

often elms, with the house placed in the shelter of any great tree that happens to be there. There may be a great walnut, an ash, a hickory, a few pin oaks, a few swamp white oaks or even an elm, that can influence the placing of the house and dominate the entire setting.

On the side of the house that faces the stream, the trees can be more gardenesque. Basswoods develop into widespread shapely trees. Mulberries, too, are delightful with their cinnamon-brown bark, irregularly cut leaves and purple, jewel-like fruit. Thorns are decorative at all times with their gray trunks, tangled branches, great thorns, white flowers, nice foliage and red fruit clusters. They can be planted much as they naturally grow—in scattered groups in the fields. They can be used, too, as hedges for the courtyard or the garden.

Many interesting stream-side shrubs can also be brought close to the house and used in groups or in unclipped hedges and hedgerows. *Viburnum Lentago* are striking with their large furry leaves, cream-white flowers and blue-black berries. Witch-hazels are tall and rigorous and especially handsome in the autumn when the leaves turn clear yellow and yellow thread-like flowers appear upon upright arching branches. The spice bushes grow naturally in groups and in loosely arranged rows. They are tall shrubs of good habit, effective all through the year. All winter their buds seem ready to open and when they do at the first call of spring the tiny yellow flowers in tight little clusters have an amazing way of simulating sunshine. The summer foliage, too, has a light-filled air and in the autumn it turns a clear sunlit yellow while the small flowers have changed into large oval glistening red berries.

Among the smaller shrubs the luxuriant green and low bushy habit of the sweet gales make them pleasant close to the house and appropriate for the edging of a terrace. Such a terrace can be the vantage point from which to look down upon the stream and its water-side garden. A winding path can lead down from it through the grass, where early flowers such as spring beauties, bloodroots, bluets and yellow adder's tongue bloom abundantly. They spread out by the hundreds and thousands, and are as delightful as naturalized daffodils. Like the daffodils, they all disappear before the grass needs cutting. Such grass may only need a few mowings or it can be left uncut so that late-blooming flowers can grow up in it and the wood ferns show their light-green fronds.

Where the path reaches the side of the stream, willows can be planted. In early spring their budding twigs show yellow and orange, in summer their foliage is gray-toned, in autumn it is fresh green amid the varied colors of the other vegetation. Under the trees trilliums can be gathered in effective groups, wild gingers can make veritable carpets, and many kinds of violets can spread out in great numbers.

The path can be made to wander along the whole length of the stream and on both sides. It can wind in and out, coming ever and again close to the water and crossing it now by a little bridge and again by stepping stones. It can pass through groups of shrubs, under trees and between flowers grown either in little clumps or in great stretches.

The dutchman's breeches grow in clumps and are doubly effective when planted under a shadbush, for both this flower and the tree have silvery foliage and white blossoms. The sweet violets, *Viola pallens,* as dainty as can be, are particularly lovely under silver maples whose silver-lined dark-green leaves flutter in every breeze. Solomon seals can be planted in clumps under the elders. They flower inconspicuously and early, before the elders become showy with large white panicles and purple fruit clusters. Swamp buttercups are scattered over the fields in great numbers and are glistening yellow. The small-flowered crowfoots grow in the same sort of places as the swamp buttercups but are simply interesting for their foliage clusters. Both of these flowers like to grow in front of red maples. Mandrakes are very effective with their decorative leaves. They grow in circular colonies or in perfect carpets under the oaks. The *Mertensia virginica* or Virginia cowslips are striking with their spires of light blue bells. They are ever so gardenesque and can be planted by the hundreds along the edge of the woods. There are many other flowers, wood anemones, Jack-in-the-pulpits, green dragons, false spikenard, false solomon's seals, early meadow-rues, bellworts and yellow oakesias. These can be offset by sensitive ferns that are decorative even in winter and early spring when

their dried fronds are still lovely and ornamented
with little dark brown fruits.

The marsh marigolds have blossoms that seem like
captured sunlight. Their bloom lasts three weeks or
more, only to give way to a light-reflecting yellow-
green foliage that stays another month before the
entire plant disappears. Marsh marigolds grow naturally in solid masses, and it is impossible to plant
too many of them. They can outline the entire stream
and be planted under willows, beside spice bushes,
below Canada plums, elms and alders. The alders
are full of interest in the early spring, for their dangling catkins hang in loose clusters all over their bold
leafless stems.

These early effects are barely over when forget-
me-nots make fairy carpets along the margins and
trail into the water. Brooklimes add their delicate
blue to the ethereal effect. Irises, too, grow just in
back of them and spread out over the sunny meadows.
There are *Iris prismatica,* the slender blue flags, and
Iris versicolor, the larger blue flag. Their flowers
rise with delicate dignity from strong underground
stems. Their gray-green sheaths accentuate the
beauty not only of the iris flowers but of the later
roses, meadow-sweets and steeple bushes. They
make a background, too, for blue lobelias, blue vervains, purplish-blue culver's roots and blue skullcaps.
These are all rather sturdy, bushy plants that flower
in summer and autumn. The brilliant blue pickerel-
weeds blossom in masses at midsummer in the water
near by and forget-me-nots linger on through the

summer months as part of an ever-varying blue scheme.

The late summer and autumn bring the gentians. They grow close to the edge of the water amid grasses and among shrubs. Fringed gentians are a soft transparent blue and come up in delicate groupings here and there. The closed gentians grow singly or in small clumps and make spots of bold opaque color. The cardinal flowers are a vivid red. When they are massed in the open their color is of startling intensity but when they are isolated and grow singly, as they often do, they seem rare and precious. They are found in the moistest spots, almost in the water.

Many other flowers bloom in the summer and autumn. Occasional rare-looking orchids are found; wild sennas with yellow butterfly flowers blossom daintily under elms, and *Chelone glabra,* the turtle-heads, are particularly lovely where they are reflected in the water in the midst of the lacy foliage of meadow rues. Arrow-heads and water lilies blossom in the quiet shallows, great cow parsnips with bold spherical flowers tower above the mud-flats, touch-me-nots blossom in moist spots, and swamp milkweeds show rich color along the water's edge. There are also joe-pye weeds that are sometimes mingled with bonesets and great asters, but are most effective when they grow by themselves in broad stretches.

In contrast to all these brilliant flowers is one effect that is particularly delicate when the virgin's bower, *Clematis virginiana,* is in flower. It grows up into the alders to cover every bush with glistening showers of starry-blossomed vines that fill the air with per-fume. The flowers later turn to feathery fruit and are beautifully offset all winter by the winter-brown alder catkins.

On a large estate, all these different plants can be assembled to vary from week to week and from season to season until spring, summer, autumn, and even winter, have each their full share of loveliness.

A small property, too, may have a little stream tumbling over rocks or a tiny brook winding through the grass or even a river frontage. Every hundred feet or less of water-side can keep its characteristic scene or have it recreated with the plants that are natural to it. On the other hand, the existing vege-tation may become the keynote. Whether it be elm or willow, sycamore or red maple, spice bush or *Viburnum Lentago,* it may suggest the character of the additional trees, shrubs, flowers and ferns that can be planted to recreate a natural scene. Each small scene, however, will be more effective when it is supplemented by adjoining ones and when together they contribute to the planting of the entire stream.

THE STREAM-SIDE ASSOCIATION

TREES

Acer Negundo ....Box Elder
Acer rubrum ....Red Maple
Acer saccharinum ....Silver Maple
Cárpinus caroliniana ....Ironwood
Carya cordiformis ....Bitter Nut
Carya glabra ....Pignut
Cary ovata ....Shag-bark Hickory
Celtis occidentalis ....Hackberry
Cratægus Crus-galli ....Hawthorn
Cratægus fecunda ....Hawthorn

TREES (*Continued*)

Fraxinus americana ....White Ash
Fraxinus nigra ....Black Ash
Fraxinus pennsylvanica ....Red Ash
Juglans cinerea ....Butternut
Juglans nigra ....Black Walnut
Liquidambar Styraciflua ....Sweet Gum
Morus rubra ....Red Mulberry
Ostrya virginiana ....Hop Hornbeam
Platanus occidentalis ....Sycamore
Populus balsamifera ....Balsam Poplar
Prunus nigra ....Canada Plum
Quercus bicolor ....Swamp White Oak
Quercus macrocarpa ....Bur Oak
Quercus palustris ....Pin Oak
Salix babylonica * ....Weeping Willow
Salix lucida ....Shining Willow
Salix nigra ....Black Willow
Tilia americana ....Basswood
Ulmus americana ....American Elm
Ulmus fulva ....Slippery Elm

SHRUBS AND VINES

Alnus incana ....Hoary Alder
Alnus rugosa ....Smooth Alder
Amelanchier canadensis ....Shad Bush
Amorpha fruticosa ....False Indigo
Benzoin aestivale ....Spice Bush
Clematis virginiana ....Virgin's Bower
Clethra alnifolia ....Sweet Pepperbush
Cornus Amomum ....Kinnikinnik
Cornus stolonifera ....Red-osier Dogwood
Hamamelis virginiana ....Witch-hazel
Ilex verticillata ....Black Alder
Menispermum canadense ....Moonseed
Myrica Gale ....Sweet Gale
Physocarpus opulifolius ....Nine-bark
Psedera quinquefolia ....Woodbine
Rosa carolina ....Rose
Rosa virginiana ....Rose
Salix cordata ....Willow
Salix discolor ....Willow
Sambucus canadensis ....Elder
Solanum Dulcamara * ....Bittersweet
Spiræa latifolia ....Meadow-sweet
Spiræa tomentosa ....Steeple Bush
Staphylea trifolia ....Bladdernut
Viburnum acerifolium ....Arrow-wood

The Stream-side

Viburnum dentatum ....Arrow-wood
Viburnum Lentago ....Nannyberry
Vitis cordifolia ....Frost Grape
Vitis vulpina ....River Bank Grape

HERBS

Acorus Calamus ....Sweet Flag
Alisma Plantago-aquatica ....Water Plantain
Anemone quinquefolia ....Wood Anemone
Angelica atropururea ....Angelica
Arisaema Dracontium ....Green Dragon
Arisaema triphyllum ....Jack-in-the-Pulpit
Asarum canadense ....Wild Ginger
Asclepias incarnata ....Swamp Milkweed
Aster lateriflorus ....Aster
Aster paniculatus ....Aster
Aster puniceus ....Aster
Aster vimineus ....Aster
Caltha palustris ....Marsh Marigold
Campanula aparinoides ....Marsh Bell-flower
Cassia marilandica ....Wild Senna
Chelone glabra ....Turtlehead
Chrysosplenium americanum ....Golden Saxifrage
Claytonia virginica ....Spring Beauty
Clematis virginiana ....Virgin's Bower
Convolvulus sepium ....Hedge Bindweed
Dentaria diphylla ....Toothwort
Dentaria laciniata ....Toothwort
Dicentra Cucullaria ....Dutchman's Breeches
Dioscorea villosa ....Wild Yam-root
Echinocystis lobata ....Wild Balsam-apple
Erythronium americanum ....Yellow Adder's Tongue
Eupatorium perfoliatum ....Boneset
Eupatorium purpureum ....Joe-Pye Weed
Gentiana Andrewsii ....Closed Gentian
Gentiana crinita ....Fringed Gentian
Geranium maculatum ....Cranesbill
Habenaria lacera ....Ragged Fringed Orchis
Habenaria psychodes ....Fringed Orchis
Helenium autumnale ....Sneezeweed
Heracleum lanatum ....Cow Parsnip
Hibiscus Moscheutos ....Swamp Rose Mallow
Houstonia caerulea ....Bluets
Humulus Lupulus ....Common Hop
Hypericum Ascyron ....Great St. John's-wort
Hypericum canadense ....St. John's-wort
Impatiens biflora ....Spotted Touch-me-not

American Plants for American Gardens

Impatiens pallida	Pale Touch-me-not
Iris prismatica	Slender Blue Flag
Iris versicolor	Larger Blue Flag
Lilium canadense	Wild Yellow Lily
Lilium philadelphicum	Wood Lily
Lobelia cardinalis	Cardinal-flower
Lobelia siphilitica	Great Lobelia
Lysimachia Nummularia *	Moneywort
Mentha piperita *	Peppermint
Mentha spicata *	Spearmint
Mertensia virginica	Virginia Cowslip
Mikania scandens	Climbing Hemp-weed
Myosotis laxa	Forget-me-not
Myosotis scorpioides *	True Forget-me-not
Oakesia sessilifolia	Oakesia
Orobanche uniflora	One-flowered Cancer-root
Peltandra virginica	Arrow Arum
Petasites palmatus	Sweet Coltsfoot
Podophyllum peltatum	May Apple
Polygonatum biflorum	Small Solomon's Seal
Polygonatum commutatum	Great Solomon's Seal
Polygonium Convolvulus	Black Bindweed
Polygonium scandens	Climbing False Buckwheat
Pontederia cordata	Pickerel-weed
Ranunculus abortivus	Small-flowered Crowfoot
Ranunculus septentrionalis	Swamp Buttercup
Rudbeckia laciniata	Cone-flower
Sagittaria latifolia	Arrow-head
Sanguinaria canadensis	Bloodroot
Scutellaria galericulata	Skullcap
Scutellaria lateriflora	Mad-dog Skullcap
Sicyos angulatus	One-seeded Bur Cucumber
Sisyrinchium angustifolium	Blue-eyed Grass
Sisyrinchium gramineum	Blue-eyed Grass
Sium cicutaefolium	Water Parsnip
Smilacena racemosa	False Spikenard
Smilacena stellata	False Solomon's Seal
Smilax herbacea	Green Brier
Smilax rotundifolia	Green Brier
Solidago Elliottii	Golden-rod
Spiranthes Romanzoffiana	Ladies' Tresses
Steironema ciliatum	Steironema
Symphytum officinale *	Common Comfrey
Thalictrum dioicum	Early Meadow Rue
Thalictrum polygamum	Tall Meadow Rue
Thaspium aureum	Meadow Parsnip
Trillium cernuum	Wake Robin

The Stream-side

HERBS (Continued)

Trillium erectum ....Wake Robin
Trillium grandiflorum ....Wake Robin
Uvularia grandiflora ....Bellwort
Uvularia perfoliata ....Bellwort
Veratum viride ....False Hellebore
Verbena hastata ....Blue Vervain
Veronica americana ....American Brooklime
Veronica Anagallis-aquatica ....Water Speedwell
Veronica virginica ....Culver's Root
Viola blanda ....Violet
Viola cucullata ....Violet
Viola pallens ....Sweet Violet
Viola scabriuscula ....Smooth Yellow Violet
Viola sororia ....Violet

FERNS

Aspidium cristatum ....Shield Fern
Aspidium noveboracense ....Shield Fern
Aspidium spinulosum ....Shield Fern
Aspidium Thelypteris ....Shield Fern
Cystopteris fragilis ....Bladder Fern
Onoclea sensibilis ....Sensitive Fern
Onoclea Struthiopteris ....Ostrich Fern
Osmunda cinnamomea ....Cinnamon Fern
Osmundo Claytoniana ....Flowering Fern
Osmunda regalis ....Flowering Fern
Woodwardia virginica ....Chain Fern

CHAPTER X

THE POND

AQUATICS are plants that thrive in quiet water and full sunlight. Many kinds of native aquatics, water shields, water lilies and water crowfoots, arrowheads, pickered-weeds, arrow arums and water plantains, sweet flags, wild callas, bur-reeds, sedges, rushes and cat-tails can be effectively used in planting a water garden.

This planting may be started with cat-tails. Their erect sheaths and reed-like stalks can edge the water and grow out into it in strong phalanxes. *Typha latifolia,* the common cat-tail, with broad leaves and stout spikes, is in scale with large ponds, while the less familiar *Typha angustifolia,* with narrow grass-like leaves and thin cylindrical spikes, is better for small places. Both of these grow among the rounded hummocks of the rushes and among the needle-like foliage of the sedges.

The sweet flags grow in shallow water. The leaves are linear, similar to the cat-tail foliage and have cone-shaped spadixes covered with numerous yellow flowers.

The bur-reeds grow in shallow water, but creep farther and farther toward the middle of the pond each year. Their Greek-formed name, *Sparganium,* alludes to their ribbon-shaped leaves that are much like the old-fashioned spiderwort. Their flowers are inconspicuous, similar to those of the grasses, but they change into very interesting fruit. The pistillate flowers that grow on the lower part of the stem change into balls of small nut-like seeds that bristle with spines, while the staminate flowers change to smaller balls of the same kind that make charming repeats above them.

All these plants have to be kept in check. Moreover, only a limited quantity of each can be used, for there must be room for the other aquatics. Beyond them in slightly deeper water are arrow-heads, pickerel-weeds and arrow arums. The arrow-heads are so ornamental that it is hardly possible to use too many of them. They should be assembled in small rather than in large groups so that the real loveliness of each tall straight stem, of each shapely leaf, of each whorl of triple blossoms, of each pure white sepal touched with lilac, may be enjoyed. The pickerel-weeds, on the other hand, gain in effectiveness when they are gathered in solid masses, for the intense blue of the flowers is only brought out when they grow close together in great quantity. The arrow arums can be used more sparingly, for they are less effective than either arrow-heads or pickerel-weeds, but they have long green curled-up spathes and green fruits that are interesting.

Among these plants water plantains may be grown. Their foliage is thick and heavily veined with the plants always scattered lightly here and there. The flowers that cover their numerous little branches are as delicate as baby's breath and accentuate their airiness.

Within this setting of arrow-heads, pickerel-weeds, arrow arums and water plantains, water shields, yellow pond lilies and sweet-scented water lilies can be planted. The water shields are dainty plants with inconspicuous thalictrum-like flowers. Their tiny, thin, water-lily-like leaves curl up on the edges so as to show their undersides and are assembled so loosely that it is possible to look down between the leaves and see the charming arrangement of the slender stems that are put into gentle movement by the slightest ripple.

In contrast to these little water shields the leaves of the yellow pond lily are not only larger but very thick and leathery. They grow in compact mats with stiff thick flower stalks that rise through them well up out of the water, often a foot or more above the leaf-covered surface, with boldly modeled, brilliantly gold flowers. The sweet-scented water lilies are quite different, with their many-petaled yellow-stamened white flowers that lie directly on the surface of the water. They grow so well that they are likely to cover the entire pond, but their real charm is accentuated when the plants are kept in small irregular groups so that the leaves can make decorative patterns upon the water and the flowers can seem like ornaments.

There are also water crowfoots; the common white water crowfoot, *Ranunculus aquatilis,* with glistening yellow stamens, the stiff water crowfoot, *Ranunculus circinatus,* with white flowers, and the yellow water crowfoot, *Ranunculus delphinifolius,* that has submerged delphinium-like leaves. All of these crowfoots have the daintiest strawberry-like blossoms that cover the water in June. After they have bloomed the plants seem lost, for they withdraw from sight under the water. This is unusual, for the main effect of aquatic plants depends upon their leaves of which there are many different kinds,—long linear sheaths, grass-like forms, shields and sagitate shapes. The sagitate leaves with their fine differentiations between the bright green slender leaves of the arrow arums, the glossy thick cordated leaves of the pickerel-weeds, and the thin, sharply pointed leaves that give the name to the arrow-heads, give a special beauty to the water garden.

The recreating of such a garden depends, first of all, upon the careful consideration of water depths, for the location of each plant is controlled by it. As the pond bed is usually saucer-shaped, the plants are arranged into a series of interlaced zones with water shields and water lilies growing in the deepest parts near the center and the cat-tails standing in the muddy shallows on the edge. This natural composition of the plants is significant.

It is necessary, too, to give the recreated water garden a situation that is convincingly appropriate. Such positions can be found in many low-lying fields, in meadows and in sunken places in woods, in fact in any natural hollow or gentle depression. Ponds may be made with comparative ease, for it is often possible to widen a little stream that flows quietly through a property, to dig out the ground below a little spring, or to use a sunken place that holds water persistently after every rain. A real feeling for contours makes it possible to keep each little depression, instead of filling it in, and to transform it into an attractive spot where aquatics naturally grow. With a sensitive appreciation of topography the outlines of the new water garden can be adapted to the existing landscape and the edges can be made to slope gently down to the water.

Such a water garden can be adapted both to a large estate and to a small place. On a property of extensive area a pond can be placed far afield where it can be gazed upon from a distance and require a little journey for a closer view of its plants. It can even be hidden away beyond a woods where it can be kept as secret as can be. On the other hand, it can often be placed quite close to the house, in fact, just below it, wherever the house itself is informal enough to be in character with such naturalistic treatment. On a small place the water garden is of necessity near the house and in sight of the porches and windows.

The path made to wind down from the house to the pond can be edged with plants like violets and forget-me-nots, irises and closed gentians, meadow-rues, turtle-heads and royal ferns, that are an introduction to the water garden itself. The pond can be encircled by a path, too, so that it can be seen from all sides and every flower beauty, every leaf texture,

The Pond

every leaf pattern can be noticed in detail. Many moisture-loving shrubs and trees; alders, button-bushes and hawthorns; clammy azaleas, sweet pepper-bushes and pin oaks; winterberry and red maples; arrow-woods and sour gums; spice bushes and elms, can be used as a background. But where the natural scene beyond is full of beauty, a single willow will sometimes be sufficient at the edge of the water.

THE POND ASSOCIATION

TREES

Acer rubrum ....Red Maple
Nyssa sylvatica ....Sour Gum
Quercus palustris ....Pin Oak
Salix nigra ....Black Willow

SHRUBS

Alnus incana ....Hoary Alder
Alnus rugosa ....Smooth Alder
Benzoin aestivale ....Spice Bush
Cephalanthus occidentalis ....Buttonbush
Clematis virginiana ....Clematis
Clethra alnifolia ....Sweet Pepperbush
Cornus Amomum ....Kinnikinnik
Cornus stolonifera ....Red-osier Dogwood
Crataegus Crus-galli ....Hawthorn
Crataegus fecunda ....Hawthorn
Gaylussacia baccata ....Black Huckleberry
Gaylussacia dumosa ....Dwarf Huckleberry
Ilex laevigata ....Smooth Winterberry
Ilex verticillata ....Winterberry
Myrica Gale ....Sweet Gale
Potentilla fruticosa ....Shrubby Cinquefoil
Pyrus arbutifolia var. *atropurpurea* ....Chokeberry
Pyrus melanocarpa ....Chokeberry
Quercus ilicifolia ....Black Scrub Oak
Rhododendron viscosum ....Clammy Azalea
Ribes oxyacanthoides var. *calcicola* ....Smooth Gooseberry
Rosa carolina ....Rose
Rosa nitida ....Rose
Rosa virginiana ....Rose
Rubus hispidus ....Blackberry

SHRUBS (*Continued*)

Salix balsamifera .... Willow
Salix candida .... Hoary Willow
Salix cordata .... Willow
Salix discolor .... Glaucous Willow
Salix glaucophylla .... Willow
Salix lucida .... Shining Willow
Salix petiolaris .... Willow
Salix sericea .... Silky Willow
Salix serissima .... Autumn Willow
Sambucus canadensis .... Common Elder
Smilax herbacea .... Carrion-flower
Smilax rotundifolia .... Common Green Brier
Solanum Dulcamara * .... Bittersweet
Spiræa latifolia .... Meadow-sweet
Spiræa tomentosa .... Steeple Bush
Vaccinium corymbosum .... High Blueberry
Viburnum dentatum .... Arrow-wood

HERBS

Acorus Calamus .... Sweet Flag
Alisma Plantago-aquatica .... Water Plantain
Arisaema triphyllum .... Jack-in-the-Pulpit
Asclepias incarnata .... Swamp Milkweed
Aster lateriflorus .... Aster
Aster novæ-angliæ .... Aster
Aster paniculatus .... Aster
Aster puniceus .... Aster
Aster vimineus .... Aster
Barbarea vulgaris .... Yellow Rocket
Brasenia Schreberi .... Water Shield
Caltha palustris .... Marsh Marigold
Campanula aparinoides .... Marsh Bell-flower
Carex sp. .... Sedge
Castalia odorata .... Sweet-scented Water Lily
Cerastium nutans .... Chickweed
Ceratophyllum demersum .... Hornwort
Chelone glabra .... Turtlehead
Chrysosplenium americanum .... Golden Saxifrage
Cicuta bulbifera .... Water Hemlock
Cicuta maculata .... Spotted Cowbane
Conioselinum chinense .... Hemlock Parsley
Elodea canadensis .... Water-weed
Epilobium molle .... Willow-herb
Eriocaulon articulatum .... Pipewort
Eriophorum gracile .... Cotton Grass
Eupatorium perfoliatum .... Boneset
Eupatorium purpureum .... Joe-Pye Weed

[94]

The Pond

Herbs (Continued)

Gentiana Andrewsii .... Closed Gentian
Gentiana crinita .... Fringed Gentian
Helenium autumnale .... Sneezeweed
Heracleum lanatum .... Cow Parsnip
Hydrocotyle americana .... Water Pennywort
Hypericum boreale .... St. John's-wort
Hypericum punctatum .... St. John's-wort
Hypericum virginicum .... Marsh St. John's-wort
Iris prismatica .... Slender Blue Flag
Iris versicolor .... Larger Blue Flag
Juncus effusus .... Common Rush
Juncus marginatus .... Rush
Lemna minor .... Duckweed
Lemna trisulca .... Duckweed
Lobelia cardinalis .... Cardinal-flower
Lobelia siphilitica .... Great Lobelia
Ludvigia alternifolia .... Seedbox
Lycopus virginicus .... Bugle Weed
Lysimachia Nummularia * .... Moneywort
Lysimachia producta .... Loosestrife
Lythrum alatum .... Loosestrife
Mikania scandens .... Climbing Hemp-weed
Mimulus ringens .... Monkey Flower
Myosotis laxa .... Forget-me-not
Myriophyllum Farwellii .... Water Milfoil
Myriophyllum spicatum .... Water Milfoil
Najas flexilis .... Naiad
Nymphaea advena .... Yellow Pond Lily
Orontium aquaticum .... Golden Club
Peltandra virginica .... Arrow Arum
Penthorum sedoides .... Ditch Stonecrop
Polygonum acre .... Water Smartweed
Polygonum amphibium .... Knotweed
Polygonum arifolium .... Halbert-leaved Tear-thumb
Polygonum Hydropiper .... Common Swartweed
Polygonum Muhlenbergii .... Knotweed
Polygonum pennsylvanicum .... Knotweed
Polygonum Persicaria * .... Lady's Thumb
Polygonum sagittatum .... Arrow-leaved Tear-thumb
Pontederia cordata .... Pickerel-weed
Potamogeton alpinus .... Pondweed
Potamogeton americanus .... Pondweed
Potamogeton heterophyllus .... Pondweed
Potamogeton Hilii .... Pondweed
Potamogeton lucens .... Pondweed
Potamogeton natans .... Pondweed
Potamogeton pectinatus .... Pondweed

[95]

Herbs (*Continued*)

Potamogeton perfoliatus	Pondweed
Potamogeton Robbinsii	Pondweed
Potamogeton zosterifolius	Pondweed
Potentilla palustris	Marsh Five-finger
Proserpinaca palustris	Mermaid-weed
Radicula aquatica	Lake Cress
Ranunculus abortivus	Small-flowered Crowfoot
Ranunculus aquatilis	Common White Water Crowfoot
Ranunculus circinatus	Stiff Water Crowfoot
Ranunculus delphinifolius	Yellow Water Crowfoot
Ranunculus recurvatus	Hooked Buttercup
Ranunculus septentrionalis	Swamp Buttercup
Sagittaria latifolia	Arrow-head
Saxifraga pennsylvanica	Swamp Saxifrage
Scutellaria galericulata	Skullcap
Scutellaria lateriflora	Mad-dog Skullcap
Senecio aureus	Golden Ragwort
Solidago Elliotii	Golden-rod
Sparganium americanum	Bur-reed
Sparganium americanum var. *androcladum*	Bur-reed
Sparganium eurycarpum	Bur-reed
Sparganium lucidum	Bur-reed
Sparganium minimum	Bur-reed
Spirodela polyrhiza	Duckweed
Symplocarpus foetidus	Skunk Cabbage
Thalictrum polygamum	Tall Meadow Rue
Thaspium aureum	Meadow Parsnip
Typha angustifolia	Cat-tail
Typha latifolia	Cat-tail
Utricularia minor	Smaller Bladderwort
Utricularia vulgaris	Greater Bladderwort
Vallisneria spiralis	Tape Grass
Verbena hastata	Blue Vervain
Verbena urticaefolia	White Vervain
Vernonia noveboracensis	Ironweed
Veronica serpyllifolia	Thyme-leaved Speedwell
Viola conspersa	Violet
Viola cucullata	Violet
Viola pallens	Sweet White Violet
Viola papilionacea	Violet
Viola sororia	Violet
Wolffia columbiana	Wolffia

Ferns

Aspidium cristatum	Shield Fern
Aspidium Thelypteris	Shield Fern
Equisetum palustre	Horsetail

The Pond

FERNS (*Continued*)

Onoclea sensibilis ....Sensitive Fern
Osmunda cinnamomea ....Cinnamon Fern
Osmunda Claytoniana ....Flowering Fern
Osmunda regalis ....Flowering Fern
Selaginella apus ....Selaginella
Woodwardia virginica ....Chain Fern

CHAPTER XI

THE BOG

A TYPICAL bog is a perfect circle with the plants arranged according to a definite plan into a series of concentric zones. In the very middle there is often a pool of water which is surrounded by a broad band of sphagnum. This moss is springy and spongy and so treacherously unstable that it is dangerous even to try to step upon it. It is difficult to tell how deep it is. Sometimes it is a thin layer, barely a foot thick, that seems to float on the top of the water. Then again it is a soft mat of unmeasurable thickness. This sphagnum is moisture-laden. It is bronze-toned and spread with the bronze-toned streamers of trailing cranberries. It forms a groundwork for the other plants. Here the buckbeans spread their dark shining leaves. They have tiny star-like velvety-white blossoms in the spring. Here the golden clubs of the *Orontium aquaticum* grow out of bunches of turquoise blue leaves and look like golden markers. The cotton grass is everywhere and has flowers whose cream-toned silken puffs are so airily attached to long slender stalks that they look as if they had just alighted there. And strange as it may seem, there are tiny seedling-like red maples scattered all over.

Then there are diminutive sundews, the famous

little fly-catchers, decorative little plants that have circlets of tiny leaves with bristly glands that glisten. They are often found around *Sarracenia purpurea,* the pitcher plant. This has clusters of pitcher-like, water-filled leaves, from which thin erect flower stalks rise a foot or two and are terminated by solitary globose closed flowers so large and heavy that they droop. The whole plant is like a sculptured ornament and is overlaid with bronze and purple coloring. Besides there are the tiny rare-looking rose pogonias with an elusive perfume, exquisite coloring, and very dainty modeling.

This flower-strewn sphagnum garden is surrounded by a ring of low shrubs. Sheep laurels, pale laurels and clammy azaleas, leather leaf and bog rosemaries, all about the same height, intermingle and form a nicely ordered compact border.

All these shrubs have lovely blossoms. The sheep laurels have rose-toned flowers and the pale laurels crimson flowers that are placed on laterally arranged pedicels scattered loosely among the leaves. The azaleas have clusters of large white flowers with tubular glandular-covered corollas. The leather leaf has glossy white flowers that hang in single file along the undersides of the stems, and the bog rosemaries have flowers that droop in little clusters from the axils of the leaves.

The refinement of these plants is just as noticeable when they are without blossoms, for they all have small leaves of astonishing beauty. The leaves of the sheep laurels are evergreen of a soft tone, while the

[99]

pale laurels have even lighter foliage with undersides
that are gray-white with a bloom. The foliage of
the clammy azaleas is rough and hairy. The dull-
toned leather leaf leaves are relieved by a sprinkle of
fine scurf. The bog rosemary has the daintiest leaves
of all. Their slenderness, their very stiffness and
their spacing far apart on the stems gives them the
utmost distinction. Moreover their curled-up edges
make them seem even narrower than they are, while
the pubescent undersides are so pale gray that they
give a gray-green tone to the whole plant.

This gray-green is repeated by the larches that
grow singly here and there at the very edge of the
border. They are slender trees. The light showing
through the loose framework gives an atmospheric
mistiness to their light green needle clusters, spaced
far apart upon black twigs. The whole effect of the
trees is noticeably airy.

It is the larches that attract attention to the bog
from far away. The only way to reach them and
the bog itself is by going across the meadow, passing
gray birch copses and thickets of arrow-woods and
high blueberries. In their midst hummocks over-
grown with osmunda ferns and black alders rise out
of little pools of dark water. It is a dangerous journey. Only the most adventurous descend into the
hollow and get a close view of the trees and the bog
itself. And only they know what an enchanted place
full of rare shrubs and flowers lies hidden there
within the thicket-surrounded fastness. It is, to be
sure, almost unbelievable that such an undrained place

The Bog

can be a unique and gardenesque spot. Yet, it is true
that this water-logged situation has all these excep-
tional plants. It is surprising that here in the water
the gray birches thrive. They are usually found in
the dryest situations. The red maples also grow here
but they are dwarfed and look like seedlings; else-
where they would have grown into slender trees. All
the shrubs, too, have thick leathery leaves as if they
were made to withstand constant lack of water. And,
in truth, all the plants are really braving severe
drought, physiological drought it is called, for the
acidity of the bog is so great that it is difficult for
them to obtain a sufficient supply of water.

This very difficulty makes a bog a garden that will
always be rare, for only a place of extensive acreage
can allow such an area to be left undrained. There,
far from the house, this fascinating group of plants
can be preserved or a bog may even be created with
all the plants assembled in concentric zones about its
water-drenched sphagnum.

THE BOG ASSOCIATION

TREES

Acer rubrum ....Red Maple
Betula populifolia ....Gray Birch
Larix laricina ....American Larch
Quercus palustris ....Pin Oak
Ulmus americana ....American Elm

SHRUBS

Amelanchier spicata ....Juneberry
Andromeda glaucophylla ....Bog Rosemary
Betula pumila ....Swamp Birch
Chamaedaphne calyculata ....Leather Leaf
Gaylussacia baccata ....Black Huckleberry

American Plants for American Gardens

SHRUBS (Continued)

Ilex verticillata ....Black Alder
Kalmia angustifolia ....Sheep Laurel
Kalmia polifolia ....Pale Laurel
Lyonia ligustrina ....Male Berry
Rhododendron viscosum ....Clammy Azalea
Rubus triflorus ....Dwarf Raspberry
Salix candida ....Hoary Willow
Salix discolor ....Glaucous Willow
Vaccinium corymbosum ....High Blueberry
Vaccinium corymbosum var. pallidum ..High Blueberry
Vaccinium macrocarpon ....Large Cranberry
Vaccinium Oxycoccos ....Small Cranberry
Viburnum dentatum ....Arrow-wood

HERBS

Arisaema triphyllum ....Jack-in-the-Pulpit
Cicuta bulbifera ....Water Hemlock
Cypripedium acaule ....Stemless Lady's Slipper
Decodon verticillatus ....Water Willow
Drosera rotundifolia ....Round-leaved Sundew
Eriophorum callitrix ....Hare's Tail
Eriophorum tenellum ....Cotton Grass
Galium palustre ....Bedstraw
Galium triflorum ....Sweet-scented Bedstraw
Geum rivale ....Purple Avens
Lysimachia terrestris ....Loosestrife
Lysimachia thrysiflora ....Tufted Loosestrife
Maianthemum canadense ....Maianthemum
Menyanthes trifolia ....Buckbean
Orontium aquaticum ....Golden Club
Pogonia ophioglossoides ....Pogonia
Potentilla palustris ....Marsh Five-finger
Sarracenia purpurea ....Pitcher Plant
Sium cicutaefolium ....Water Parsnip
Thalictrum dioicum ....Meadow Rue
Typha latifolia ....Cat-tail
Viola conspersa ....Violet
Viola pallens ....Sweet White Violet

FERNS

Aspidium cristatum ....Shield Fern
Aspidium spinulosum ....Shield Fern
Aspidium Thelypteris ....Shield Fern
Equisetum palustre ....Horsetail
Onoclea sensibilis ....Sensitive Fern
Osmunda regalis ....Flowering Fern

[102]

CHAPTER XII

THE SEASIDE

ALONG the North Atlantic coast with its far look to sea and with its great sweep of the sky, with its shelving rocks, undulating dunes and sandy flats, a small group of trees, shrubs and flowers grows with rugged vigor.

Here pitch pines are the stalwart trees. Their stout trunks, rough bark, angular branches and short needles make it possible for them to hold their own valiantly. The early settlers found them in great forests on the high cliffs of Maine, on the shores of Massachusetts, Connecticut, Long Island, New Jersey, in fact all along the coast as far south as Georgia. In some places pitch pines still make an evergreen background for the shore, in other places only a few scraggly trees remain. They are so noticeable, however, that this whole region is known as the pine barrens.

Oaks are almost as prominent. They grow up in the pitch-pine woods and form its principal undergrowth. Where the pines have been destroyed the oaks have become the important trees. They are never the great trees of the oak woodlands on inland ridges. Most of them are of medium size with a rough-branched picturesqueness and some are only low wind-blown scrubby bushes. There are several varieties. The black scrub oak, *Quercus ilicifolia*, thrives even among the bleak rocks of Maine. The post oak, *Quercus stellata*, braves the Massachusetts shore but grows better farther south where it mingles with the black jack oak, *Quercus marilandica*, and with the willow oak, *Quercus phellos*. Besides, there is *Quercus prinoides*, that grows with all these other species in Long Island, New Jersey and farther south.

Other trees and shrubs grow here. There are hollies and cedars, sassafrases and amelanchiers, hawthorns, and wild cherries. There are willows and hazelnuts, chokeberries and beach plums. There are *Rhus copallina*, one of the sumachs, and occasional virburnums such as *Viburnum venosum*. Then, too, there are bayberries and inkberries, and a great variety of blueberries, dangleberries and huckleberries. There are roses, *Rosa humilis, Rosa blanda, Rosa virginiana*. There are New Jersey teas and sweet ferns, *Juniperus horizontalis*, one of the low-lying prostrate junipers, and the little-known *Pyrus arbutifolia* var., *atropurpurea* which is a delightful small shrub with rose pink flowers. Besides there are woody ground covers like coremas and hudsonias, bearberries and sand myrtles, and a vigorous group of herbaceous plants.

These are the plants that have adapted themselves to the rock-bound coast and sandy shore. They have the power to cope with barren soil and excessive dryness. They can brave the winds that sweep over them from the ocean. They are storm-tossed, gale-bent, weather-gnarled. Exposure is the source of their significant beauty. Even their foliage is proof against the drying winds. Some leaves like those of the inkberries have thick leathery surfaces, some like the bayberries have a waxy bloom, and some like the willows have a hairy covering. These protective coatings, also, give the foliage its astonishing variation of tone. There is the deep green of the pines, the glossy green of the oaks, all the gray-greens of amelanchiers and bayberries, roses and beach plums, and even the more noticeable grayness of coremas and sand myrtles. This coloring is beautifully harmonious with the rocks and the sands. It is even more effective in the autumn, when the foliage turns to bronze and purple, rose and maroon.

There is something fundamental in this vegetation. It is surprising that it has ever been uprooted and that other plants have been used in its place. Its preservation retains natural settings for seaside houses. The houses themselves ought to be an integral part of the landscape. In order that this may be so, the close relationship that exists between buildings and their settings needs to be understood as the early settlers understood it when they built their houses solidly upon the windswept coast. These houses all fit the contours of the land, conform to the shelving ledges and even hide themselves in the undulations of the dunes. Their exteriors, whether they be of native stone, broad clapboards, or shingles, are harmonious in coloring, in feeling, in origin even, with their environment.

The first place to reëstablish the native vegetation is in defining the boundaries of the property. Roses, together with meadow-sweets and steeple bushes, can be grown in narrow borders about the smallest plot or in broad masses around the largest place. They are appropriate for both a cottage and a great rambling country house. For more rugged plantations hazels can be used. They have long been associated with gardens. Chokeberries make tall thick shrubberies. They have shiny foliage, hawthorn-like white flowers and little clusters of small red berries. Beach plums that cling tenaciously to sandy slopes, have low, sweeping branches that make them good for informal hedgings. But of all these plants the bayberries are best, not only because their rounded compact forms naturally make hedge-like formations, but because their silhouettes, their foliage, their gray waxy fruit, in fact the whole feeling of the plant, fits these surroundings.

None of these plants should be arranged in the usual stiff, straight hedges. They should be planted irregularly to blend with the undulating contours. If possible, several varieties should be used. Roses and blueberries, bayberries and dangleberries with groups of cherries and of sassafrases, of cedars, a few oaks and even an occasional pine will make a real hedgerow.

All these plants can, too, be brought up to the house. Their rugged forms adapt them to architectural masses. Bayberries, for instance, can be planted right against the house. They are rather difficult to move, except in small sizes, but they have an astonishing adaptability. Sometimes, in very exposed places, they remain low like ground-covers and again in sheltered positions they become great rounded bushes, eight feet high or more, fine enough in form and foliage to be planted as accents beside the main entrance. Low plants, like *Pyrus arbutifolia* var. *atropurpurea,* roses, and inkberries can be planted under the windows. Blueberries can be used against wall spaces. They have fascinatingly angular twiggage. wonderful foliage, and delicate white flowers. Crabs and hawthorns can be planted in groups to shelter the porch and terrace. Their flowers are as exquisite as the English May, their berries are a brilliant red, and their irregular forms make fascinating silhouettes against the house.

Such planting can be carried out from the house so as to cover the exposed stretches that slope down to the water. Low thickets of sweet fern and roses, bayberries, and huckleberries can be planted in the luxuriant way they naturally grow, with here and there an accenting group of taller shrubs and trees. And every blueberry bush, every oak, every pine that is growing there can be preserved to add a characteristic picturesqueness to the scene.

Such planting leaves no room for a lawn. In fact a lawn would be quite out of place. It has an unnatural look among the out-cropping rocks. It becomes sun-scorched and wind-dried. There are however, many natural grasses that stay green during the hot summer and then turn to tan and tawny tones

in the fall. They are not too rough. Some, like the
beard grass, are rather nicely tufted and make quite
an even turf, while the rest are smooth enough to
walk upon.

The paths that wander through these grasses and
thickets can lead to gardens of native trees, shrubs
and flowers. Pines wherever they exist can make the
dark green background to the whole scene and hollies
can be used as telling accents. The hollies do not grow
as far north as Boston but they grow well in Long
Island and in New Jersey as well as farther south.
They are, to be sure, very slow growing. Like the
pines they are extremely difficult to transplant. Rather
large sized specimens are occasionally moved with
success but even small trees are well worth transplant-
ing for they are very decorative. Their scarlet berries make the tree a mid-winter wonder, and the shining foliage makes them effective throughout the year.
With the pines and hollies some of the heaths can be
effectively used. Pyxies, bearberries and sand myrtles
can be planted as edgings and ground covers. The
pyxie, or flowering moss, is a tiny plant that creeps
close along the ground. It is really elfin-like when it
is covered with little starry flowers. In some places
the arbutus establishes itself with the pixies. The
bearberries are lovely too. They spread the ground
with carpets of shining evergreen leaves that shelter
little urn-shaped white flowers. And the sand myrtles,
or *Leiophyllum buxifolia,* are perhaps the most exquisite of them all. They are only a few inches high.

Their little branches have oval myrtle-like leaves and umbels of small white heath-like flowers. These plants blossom in the spring but their evergreen foliage make even summer use of them full of interest. In back of these small edgings evergreen sheep laurels with their rose-red flowers and the inkberries with their small leathery leaves can be inter-planted, and with these blueberries and huckleberries, for these plants together make a fascinating heath garden.

Most of the gardens should, however, be closer to the house, beside the porch or outside the living room. These gardens need not be gardens in the ordinary sense of the word. They need not be laid out in geometric shapes that relate their beds and borders, their paths and hedges to the straight lines of the house. They can be informal with planting that is arranged to fit the contours of the land and to make the most of rocky outcrops and sandy hollows. They can be tucked away within enclosures of beach plums, hawthorns, cherries or amelanchiers. The amelanchiers are, perhaps, the loveliest of all. Their soft silvery-white flowers cover their drooping leafless branches in foamy masses early in the spring. Their foliage is enjoyable all summer long. They can form a background for an intimate garden of the most delicate seaside flowers. The borders can be edged with hudsonias that cover their dense little tufts with heath-like flowers or with the heather that has become naturalized in many places. Or edgings can be made of *Corema conradii,* whose foliage is sage green and whose whorls of white bells are of exquisite workmanship. Then, rare-looking flaxes can be used in slender drifts, spiranthes or ladies' tresses in nice little groupings, gerardias in fascinating numbers. And masses of striking wild lupines, beach-pea, lespedezas, and adorable low blue asters with grassy foliage can be planted. These alone would make a blue garden as lovely as can be. A gayer garden, too, can be made, all of yellow flowers, with rock-roses, hypericums, and evening primroses, with golden-rods and the golden *Chryopsis falcata* that continues its summer bloom well into the autumn and crowds its much-branched clumps with bright aster-like flowers. Besides these, little accents of wild indigo can be added and little clusters of *Tephrosia virginiana*. This is the hoary pea or goat's rue that has fine compound leaves and pea-like yellow flowers with crimson keels. Here is bright color as up-to-date as you wish. A garden where burnt-orange butterfly-weed and orange-scarlet *Lilium philadelphicum* are intermingled would be even more fascinating and sufficient for mid-summer. The combination is astonishingly modern and particularly effective when it is near a silvery-gray house or against a background of cedar. All these flowers are particularly brilliant in the sunlight of the seaside but there is no crudity in the effect. The foliage helps to harmonize them with the sands, the rocks and the sea.

That is why these flowers are effective when they are grown right out in the open and allowed to spread freely over the rocks and the sand. There are so many delightful ground covers, too, like *Cerastium arvense* that, for all its chickweed habits, makes a dainty spring effect with a profusion of starry flowers. It is especially delightful when it grows with the bird-foot violets. And there is the sand grass and *Polygonella articulata* and *Arenaria peploides.* These grow even in beach sand. The sandwort has flowers that sometimes are deep rose and sometimes white. The *Polygonella articulata* has foliage of yellow green that livens the sand. And then there is the curious prickly pear, *Opuntia vulgaris,* with its cactus-like leaves. Its clear yellow flowers are delicately formed as of spun glass and have a sheen like a rose. The hudsonias, too, grow in great masses over rock and sand. Many different everlastings like these situations. Even the *Corema conradii,* the bearberries and the sand myrtles grow out in the open. The spreading flatness characteristic of many of these plants offers an opportunity of trying interesting experiments. Instead of the graded heights that are used in most borders there can be an evenness of height which is better suited to exposed places and makes better foregrounds for views of the sea. Many of the plants are so low, in fact, that they are out of the direct sweep of the wind. Many, too, have billowy undulations like the dunes and the waves. They all are by their nature a part of their environment.

THE SEASIDE ASSOCIATION

TREES

Betula populifolia	Gray Birch
Carya glabra	Pignut

American Plants for American Gardens

TREES (Continued)

Carya alba ....Mocker Nut
Crataegus tomentosa ....Hawthorn
Juniperus virginiana ....Red Cedar
Liquidambar Styraciflua ....Sweet Gum
Nyssa sylvatica ....Black Gum
Pinus rigida ....Pitch Pine
Prunus serotina ....Wild Black Cherry
Quercus alba ....White Oak
Quercus coccinea ....Scarlet Oak
Quercus illicifolia ....Black Scrub Oak
Quercus marilandica ....Black Jack Oak
Quercus phellos ....Willow Oak
Quercus prinoides ....Oak
Quercus Prinus ....Chestnut Oak
Quercus rubra ....Red Oak
Quercus stellata ....Post Oak
Quercus velutina ....Black Oak

SHRUBS AND VINES

Amelanchier canadensis ....Shad Bush
Calluna vulgaris * ....Heather
Ceanothus americanus ....New Jersey Tea
Clethra alnifolia ....Sweet Pepperbush
Corylus americana ....Hazelnut
Cratægus sp. ....Hawthorn
Gaylussacia baccata ....Black Huckleberry
Gaylussacia dumosa ....Dwarf Huckleberry
Gaylussacia frondosa ....Dangleberry
Ilex glabra ....Inkberry
Ilex opaca ....American Holly
Juniperus horizontalis ....Juniper
Kalmia angustifolia ....Sheep Laurel
Lyonia mariana ....Stagger-bush
Myrica asplenifolia ....Sweet Fern
Myrica carolinensis ....Bayberry
Prunus maritima ....Beach Plum
Psedera quinquefolia ....Woodbine
Pyrus arbutifolia var. atropurpurea ....Chokeberry
Pyrus melanocarpa ....Chokeberry
Rhus copallina ....Dwarf Sumach
Rosa blanda ....Rose
Rosa humilis ....Rose
Rosa nitida ....Rose
Rosa virginiana ....Rose
Salix humilis ....Prairie Willow
Sambucus racemosa ....Elder

The Seaside

Herbs (*Continued*)

Gerardia purpurea	Purple Gerardia
Gerardia setacea	Gerardia
Gerardia virginica	Smooth False Foxglove
Gnaphalium purpureum	Purplish Cudweed
Helianthemum canadense	Rockrose
Hudsonia ericoides	Hudsonia
Hudsonia tomentosa	Hudsonia
Hypericum canadense	St. John's-wort
Hypoxis hirsuta	Star Grass
Lathyrus maritimus	Beach Pea
Lechea minor	Lechea
Lechea racemulosa	Lechea
Lechea villosa	Lechea
Leiophyllum buxifolium	Sand Myrtle
Lespedeza angustifolia	Bush Clover
Lespedeza capitata	Bush Clover
Lespedeza frutescens	Bush Clover
Lespedeza hirta	Bush Clover
Liatris elegans	Blazing Star
Liatris graminifolia	Blazing Star
Liatris squarrosa	Blazing Star
Lilium philadelphicum	Wood Lily
Linaria canadensis	Toadflax
Linum floridanum	Flax
Linum medium	Flax
Lupinus perennis	Wild Lupine
Lysimachia quadrifolia	Loosestrife
Monarda punctata	Horse Mint
Œnothera fruticosa	Sundrops
Œnothera linearis	Evening Primrose
Opuntia vulgaris	Prickly Pear
Panicum Addisonii	Panic Grass
Panicum Ashei	Panic Grass
Panicum columbianum	Panic Grass
Panicum Commonsianum	Panic Grass
Panicum depauperatum	Panic Grass
Panicum Lindheimeri	Panic Grass
Panicum oricola	Panic Grass
Panicum sphaerocarpon	Panic Grass
Panicum tsugetorum	Panic Grass
Panicum villosissimum	Panic Grass
Polygonella articulata	Polygonella
Polygonum monspeliensis	Beard Grass
Pyxidanthera barbulata	Pyxie
Solidago bicolor	Golden-rod
Solidago erecta	Golden-rod
Solidago odora	Sweet Golden-rod

The Seaside

INDEX

Index

Ash, 76, 78
Asparagus officinalis, 20
Asperula galioides, 20
Aspidium cristatum, 87, 96, 102
Aspidium marginale, 34, 38, 42, 50,
  56, 65, 68, 69, 73, 87
Aspidium noveboracense, 56, 65, 73,
  74
Aspidium spinulosum, 42, 50, 56,
  62, 65, 68, 69, 73, 87, 102
Aspidium Thelypteris, 102
Asplenium acrostichoides, 73
Asplenium Filix-femina, 65
Asplenium platyneuron, 34, 37, 38,
  56, 65, 69, 73
Asplenium Ruta-muraria, 34, 56, 69,
  73
Asplenium Trichomanes, 34, 38, 56,
  65, 69, 73
Aster, 26, 31, 32, 33, 50, 51, 54,
  85, 94, 110, 113
Aster acuminatus, 50, 54
Aster concolor, 113
Aster cordifolius, 14, 26, 32, 37, 54
Aster divaricatus, 14, 20, 54
Aster dumosus, 113
Aster ericoides, 14, 20, 26, 32
Aster gracilis, 113
Aster infirmus, 54
Aster laevis, 14, 20
Aster laterifolius, 14, 20, 85, 90
Aster linariifolius, 54
Aster macrophyllus, 14, 20, 50, 54
Aster nemoralis, 113
Aster novae-angliae, 14, 20, 32, 94
Aster novi-belgii, 113
Aster paniculatus, 14, 20, 85, 94
Aster patens, 14, 20, 113
Aster prenanthoides, 26, 33, 37, 54
Aster ptarmicoides, 14, 20
Aster puniceus, 85, 94
Aster spectabilis, 113
Aster undulatus, 113
Aster vimineus, 14, 20, 26, 33, 37,
  85, 94

Baneberry, 44, 50, 62
Baptisia tinctoria, 54, 113

Barbarea vulgaris, 20, 94
Barberry Common, 32
Basswood, 43, 63, 72, 76, 78, 84
Bayberry, 25, 32, 36, 104, 105, 107,
  112
Beach Grass, 113
Beach pea, 110, 114
Beach plum, 104, 105, 109, 112
Bean Wild, 22
Bearberry, 104, 108, 111, 113
Beard Grass, 113, 114
Beard-tongue, 22, 55
Bedstraw, 21, 102
Beech, 43, 57, 59, 60, 61, 63, 71
Beech Fern, 62, 65, 69, 73
Beech-drops, 64, 72
Bellwort, 44, 55, 58, 63, 64, 67, 71,
  80, 87
Benzoin aestivale, 84, 93
Berberis vulgaris, 25, 32
Bergamot, 13, 33
Bergamot Wild, 22
Betula alba, 63, 71
Betula lenta, 63, 71
Betula lutea, 63, 71
Betula populifolia, 37, 101, 111
Betula pumila, 101
Bindweed, 21
Birch, 61
Bird's-foot Violet, 111, 115
Bishop's Cap, 44, 51, 55, 62, 64,
  67, 72
Bitter Nut, 71, 76, 83
Bittersweet, 19, 25, 29, 32, 53, 84,
  94
Black Alder, 76, 77, 84, 100, 102
  Ash, 84
  Bindweed, 86
  Birch, 58, 59, 63, 71
  Gum, 112
  High Blueberry, 113
  Huckleberry, 93, 101, 112
  Jack Oak, 112
  Oak, 53, 112
  Scrub Oak, 93, 112
  Snakeroot, 54
  Walnut, 84
  Willow, 71, 84, 93

Index

Index

Index

[121]

Index

Index

[123]

Index

Index

Index

Index

Index

virginiensis, 33, 55, 73
Saxifrage, 30
  Early, 33
Scarlet oak, 53, 112
Scrophularia leporella, 55
Scutellaria galericulata, 86, 96
  laterflora, 86, 96
Sedge, 88, 94, 113
Sedum acre, 73
Seedbox, 95
Selaginella, 74, 97
  apus, 97
  rupestris, 69, 74
Self-heal, 33, 35, 37, 38, 55
Senecio aureus, 96
Sensitive Fern, 73, 80, 87, 97, 102
Shad Bush, 53, 64, 72, 76, 80, 84, 112
Shag-bark Hickory, 83
Sheep Laurel, 99, 109, 102, 112
Shield Fern, 56, 65, 69, 73, 87, 96, 102
Shin Leaf, 33, 55
Shining Willow, 84
Showy Orchis, 55, 64
Shrubby Cinquefoil, 93
Sicyos angulatus, 86
Silene latifolia, 22
  noctiflora, 22
Silver Maple, 76, 80, 83
Silver-rod, 33
Sisyrinchium angustifolium, 22, 86
  gramineum, 86
Sium cicutaefolium, 86, 102
Skullcap, 81, 86, 96
  Mad-dog, 96
Skunk Cabbage, 96
Slender Blue Flag, 81, 86, 95
Slippery Elm, 84
Small Cranberry, 102
Small Solomon's Seal, 55, 64, 73, 86
Smaller Bladderwort, 96
Small-flowered Crowfoot, 80, 86, 96
Smartweed Common, 95
Smilacina racemosa, 33, 55, 64, 73, 86
  stellata, 86
Smilax glauca, 113

herbacea, 86, 93
  rotundifolia, 86, 93
Smooth Alder, 72, 84, 93
Smooth False Foxglove, 55, 114
  Gooseberry, 93
  Winterberry, 93
Snakeroot black, 44, 50
Sneezeweed, 85, 95
Solanum Dulcamara, 84, 93
  nigrum, 22
Solidago altissima, 22
  bicolor, 22, 33, 38, 42, 55, 114
  caesia, 55
  canadensis, 22, 42
  Elliottii, 86, 96
  erecta, 114
  graminifolia, 22, 26, 33
  latifolia, 55
  nemoralis, 22, 26, 33
  odora, 114
  puberula, 115
  rigida, 22
  rugosa, 22, 33, 34
  sempervirens, 115
  squarrosa, 55
  stricta, 115
  tenuifolia, 115
Solomon's Seal, 44, 51, 64, 67, 70
  False, 33
  Small, 33
Sorrel Common Wood, 33, 37
  Sheep, 22
  Wood, 22
Sour Gum, 93
Spanish Buttons, 20
Sparganium, 88
  americanum, 96
  androcladum, 96
  lucidum, 96
  minimum, 96
Specularia perfoliata, 22
Speedwell, 26, 34, 37, 55
  Common, 38
Spice Bush, 76, 78, 80, 83, 84, 93
Spikenard, 44, 58
  False, 51
Spirea latifolia, 16, 20, 84, 93, 113
  tomentosa, 16, 21, 84, 93, 113

[128]

Index

Index

[130]

Index

APPENDIX

Plants included in text whose names have changed since the original publication.

CHAPTER II: THE OPEN FIELD

OLD	NEW	PAGE
	SHRUBS	
Cornus circinata	C. rugosa	19
Cornus paniculata	C. racemosa	19
Myrica asplenifolia	Comptonia peregrina	19
Prunus cuneata	P. pumila var. cuneata	19
Prunus pennsylvanica	P. pensylvanica	19
Psedera quinquefolia	Parthenocissus quinquefolia	19
Ribes vulgare	R. sativum	19
Rosa rubiginosa	R. eglanteria	19
Rubus recurvans	R. pensylvanicus	19
Rubus villosus	R. flagellaris	20
Spiraea latifolia	S. alba var. latifolia	20
Viburnum cassinoides	V. nudum var. cassinoides	20
Viburnum Lentago	V. lentago	20
Viburnum pubescens	V. rafinesquianum var. rafinesquianum	20
	HERBS	
Achillea Millefolium	A. millefolium	20
Antennaria Parlinii	A. plantaginifolia var. parlinii	20
Asperula galioides	Galium glaucum	20
Aster paniculatus	A. lanceolatus var. simplex	20
Aster ptarmicoides	Solidago ptarmicoides	20

Appendix

Appendix

FERNS

Dicksonia punctilobula	Dennstaedtia punctilobula	23

CHAPTER III: THE JUNIPER HILLSIDE

OLD	NEW	PAGE
	TREES	
Robinia Pseudo-Acacia	R. pseudoacacia	32
	SHRUBS	
Cornus paniculata	C. racemosa	32
Myrica carolinensis	M. pensylvanica	32
Myrica asplenifolia	Comptonia peregrina	32
Psedera quinquefolia	Parthenocissus quinquefolia	32
Ribes vulgare	R. sativum	32
Vaccinium pennsylvanicum	V. angustifolium	32
Virburnum Lentago	V. lentago	32
Viburnum pubescens	V. rafinesquianum	32
	var. rafinesquianum	
	HERBS	
Achillea Millefolium	A. millefolium	32
Antennaria Parlinii	A. plantaginifolia var. parlinii	32
Aster vimineus	A. racemosus	33
Chrysanthemum Leucanthemum	C. leucanthemum	33
Lespedeza simulata	Lespedeza x simulata	33
Oenothera pumila	O. perennis	33
Oxalis filipes	O. dillenii	33
Oxalis stricta	O. dillenii	33
Potentilla pumila	P. canadensis	33
Polygala pauciflora	P. paucifolia	33
Solidago graminifolia	Euthamia graminifolia	33
Verbascum Blattaria	V. blattaria	34
Viola fimbriatula	V. sagittata	34

Appendix

FERNS

Aspidium marginale	Dryopteris marginalis	34
Asplenium Ruta-muraria	A. ruta-muraria	34
Asplenium Trichomanes	A. trichomanes	34
Lycopodium obscurum	L. obscurum	34
var. dendrobium		
Polypodium vulgare	P. virginianum	34

CHAPTER IV: THE GRAY BIRCHES

OLD	NEW	PAGE

HERBS

Aster vimineus	A. racemosus	37
Lespedeza simulata	Lespedeza x simulata	37
Oxalis filipes	O. dillenii	37
Oxalis stricta	O. dillenii	37

FERNS

Aspidium marginale	Dryopteris marginalis	38
Asplenium Trichomanes	A. trichomanes	38
Polypodium vulgare	P. virginianum	38

CHAPTER V: THE PINES

OLD	NEW	PAGE

HERBS

Lespedeza simulata	Lespedeza x simulata	42

FERNS

Aspidium marginale	Dryopteris marginalis	42
Aspidium spinulosum	Dryopteris carthusiana	42
Lycopodium obscurum	L. obscurum	42
var. dendrobium		

Appendix

CHAPTER VI: THE OAK WOODS

OLD	NEW	PAGE
	TREES	
Carya alba	C. tomentosa	53
Liridendron Tulipifera	L. tulipifera	53
Prunus pennsylvanica	P. pensylvanica	53
Pyrus americana	Sorbus americana	53
Quercus Muhlenbergii	Q. muhlenbergii	53
Quercus Prinus	Q. prinus	53
Sassafras variifolium	S. albidum	53
	SHRUBS AND VINES	
Diervilla Lonicera	D. lonicera	53
Rhododendron nudiflorum	R. periclymenoides	53
Ribes Cynosbati	R. cynosbati	53
	HERBS	
Asclepias phytolaccoides	A. exaltata	54
Galium Aparine	G. aparine	54
Gerardia flava	Aureolaria virginica	55
Gerardia virginica	Aureolaria virginica	55
Hepatica triloba	H. acutiloba	55
Oakesia sessilifolia	Uvularia sessilifolia	55
Panax trifolium	Panax trifolius	55
Pentstemon laevigatus var. Digitalis	Penstemon digitalis	55
Scrophularia leporella	S. lanceolata	55
Viola triloba	V. palmata	56
	FERNS	
Aspidium noveboracense	Thelypteris noveboracensis	56
Aspidium spinulosum	Dryopteris carthusiana	56
Botrychium obliquum var. dissectum	B. dissectum	56

Appendix

Botrychium ternatum	B. biternatum	56
Camptosorus rhizophyllus	Asplenium rhizophyllum	56
Polypodium vulgare	P. virginianum	56
Polystichum acrostichoides	P. acrostichoides	56
var. Schweinitzii		

CHAPTER VII: THE BEECH-MAPLE-HEMLOCK WOODS

OLD	NEW	PAGE
	TREES	
Acer pennsylvanicum	A. pensylvanicum	63
Betula lutea	B. allegheniensis	63
Liriodendron Tulipifera	L. tulipifera	63
	SHRUBS	
Amelanchier oblongifolia	A. canadensis	64
	HERBS	
Dicentra Cucullaria	D. cucullaria	64
Eupatorium urticaefolium	E. rugosum	64
Geranium Robertianum	G. robertianum	64
Trientalis americana	T. borealis	64
Viola triloba	V. palmata	64
	FERNS	
Aspidium marginale	Dryopteris marginalis	65
Aspidium noveboracense	Thelypteris noveboracensis	65
Aspidium spinulosum	Dryopteris carthusiana	65
Asplenium Filix-femina	Athyrium felix-femina	65
Asplenium Ruta-muraria	A. ruta-muraria	65
Asplenium Trichomanes	A. trichomanes	65
Botrychium obliquum	B. dissectum	65
var. dissectum		
Botrychium ternatum	B. biternatum	65

Appendix

Camptosorus rhizophyllus	Asplenium rhizophyllum	65
Dicksonia punctilobula	Dennstaedtia punctilobula	65
Phegopteris Dryopteris	Gymnocarpium dryopteris	65
Phegopteris hexagonoptera	Thelypteris hexagonoptera	65
Phegopteris polypodioides	Thelypteris phegopteris	65
Polypodium vulgare	P. virginianum	65
Polystichum acrostichoides var. Schweinitzii	P. acrostichoides	65

CHAPTER VIII: THE HEMLOCK RAVINE

OLD	NEW	PAGE
	TREES	
Acer pennsylvanicum	A. pensylvanicum	71
Betula lutea	B. allegheniensis	71
Liriodendron Tulipifera	L. tulipifera	71
	SHRUBS	
Alnus rugosa	Alnus incana	72
Salix glaucophylla	S. myricoides	72
	HERBS	
Arisaema Dracontium	A. dracontium	72
Dicentra Cucullaria	D. cucullaria	72
Parnassia caroliniana	P. glauca	72
Trientalis americana	T. borealis	73
Trillium declinatum	T. flexipes	73
	FERNS	
Aspidium marginale	Dryopteris marginalis	73
Aspidium marginale var. elegans	Dryopteris marginalis	73
Aspidium noveboracense	Thelypteris noveboracensis	73
Asplenium acrostichoides	Athyrium thelypteroides	73

Appendix

CHAPTER NINE: THE STREAM-SIDE

Appendix

Aster vimineus	A. racemosus	85
Cassia marilandica	Senna hebecarpa	85
Convolvulus sepium	Calystegia sepium	85
Dentaria diphylla	Cardamine diphyllia	85
Dentaria laciniata	Cardamine concatenata	85
Dicentra Cucullaria	D. cucullaria	85
Gentiana Andrewsii	G. andrewsii	85
Gentiana crinita	Gentianopsis crinita	85
Hibiscus Moscheutos	H. moscheutos	85
Houstonia caerulea	Hedyotis caerulea	85
Humulus Lupulus	H. lupulus	85
Hypericum Ascyron	H. pyramidatum	85
Impatiens biflora	I. capensis	85
Lysimachia Nummularia	L. nummularia	86
Menthapiperita	Mentha x piperita	86
Oakesia sessilifolia	Uvularia sessilifolia	86
Petasites palmatus	P. frigidus	86
Polygonatum commutatum	P. biflorum	86
Polygonium Convoluulus	Polygonum convoluulus	86
Polygonium scandens	Polygonum scandens	86
Ranunculus septentrionalis	R. hispidus var. nitidus	86
Sisyrinchium gramineum	S. angustifolium	86
Sium cicutaefolium	S. suave	86
Solidago Elliottii	S. elliottii	86
Spiranthes Romanzoffiana	S. romanzoffiana	86
Steironema ciliatum	Lysimachia ciliata	86
Thalictrum polygamum	T. pubescens	86
Thaspium aureum	T. trifoliatum	86
Veronica Anagallis-aquatica	V. angallis-aquatica	87
Veronica virginica	Veronicastrum virginicum	87
Viola pallens	V. macloskeyi	87
Viola scabriuscula	V. pubescens	87

FERNS

Aspidium cristatum	Dryopteris cristata	87
Aspidium noveboracense	Thelypteris noveboracensis	87

Appendix

OLD	NEW	PAGE
Aspidium spinulosum	Dryopteris carthusiana	87
Aspidium Thelypteris	Thelypteris palustris	87
Onoclea Struthiopteris	Matteuccia struthiopteris	87
Osmunda Clatyoniana	O. claytoniana	87

CHAPTER X: THE POND

OLD	NEW	PAGE
	SHRUBS	
Alnus rugosa	Alnus incana	93
Benzoin aestivale	Lindera benzoin	93
Cornus Amomum	C. amomum	93
Cornus stolonifera	C. sericea	93
Pyrus arbutifolia var. atropurpurea	Aronia arbutifolia	93
Pyrus melanocarpa	Aronia melanocarpa	93
Ribes oxyacanthoides var. calciola	R. oxyacanthoides	93
Salix balsamifera	S. pyrifolia	94
Salix glaucophylla	S. myricoides	94
Solanum Dulcamara	S. dulcamara	94
Spiraea latifolia	S. alba var. latifolia	94
	HERBS	
Acorus Calamus	A. calamus	94
Alisma Plantago-aquatica	A. subcordatum	94
Aster paniculatus	A. lanceolatus	94
Aster vimineus	A. racemosus	94
Brasenia Schreberi	B. schreberi	94
Castalia odorata	Nymphaea odorata	94
Epilobium molle	E. strictum	94
Eriocaulon articulatum	E. aquaticum	94
Gentiana Andrewsii	G. andrewsii	95
Gentiana crinita	Gentianopsis crinita	95

Appendix

Hypericum virginicum	Triadenum virginicum	95
Lysimachia Nummularia	L. nummularia	95
Lysimachia producta	Lysimachia x producta	95
Myriophyllum Farwellii	M. farwelli	95
Nymphaea advena	Nuphar advena	95
Polygonum acre	P. punctatum	95
Polygonum Hydropiper	P. hydropiper	95
Polygonum Muhlenbergii	P. amphibium	95
Polygonum Persicaria	P. persicaria	95
Potamogeton americanus	P. nodosus	95
Potamogeton heterphyllus	P. gramineus	95
Potamogeton Hilii	P. hillii	95
Potamogeton lucens	P. illinoensis	95
Potamogeton Robbinsii	R. robbinsii	96
Potamogeton zosterifolius	P. zosteriformis	96
Radicula aquatica	Armoracia lacustris	96
Ranunculus aquatilis	R. trichophyllus	96
Ranunculus circinatus	R. subrigidus	96
Ranunculus delphinifolius	R. flabellaris	96
Ranunculus septentrionalis	R. hispidus var. nitidus	96
Saxifraga pennsylvanica	S. pensylvanica	96
Solidago Elliottii	S. elliottii	96
Sparganium lucidum	S. androcladum	96
Thalictrum polygamum	T. pubescens	96
Thaspium aureum	T. trifoliatum	96
Vallisneria spiralis	V. americana	96
Viola pallens	V. macloskeyi	96
Viola papilionacea	V. sororia	96

FERNS

Aspidium cristatum	Dryopteris cristata	96
Aspidium Thelypteris	Thelypteris palustris	96
Osmunda Claytoniana	O. claytoniana	97
Selaginella apus	S. apoda	97

Appendix

CHAPTER XI: THE BOG

OLD	NEW	PAGE
SHRUBS		
Rubus triflorus	R. pubescens	102
Vaccinium corymbosum var. pallidum	V. pallidum	102
Vaccinium Oxycoccos	V. oxycoccos	102
HERBS		
Eriophorum callitrix	E. vaginatum	102
Viola pallens	V. macloskeyi	102
FERNS		
Aspidium cristatum	Dryopteris cristata	102
Aspidium Thelypteris	Thelypteris palustris	102

CHAPTER XII: THE SEASIDE

OLD	NEW	PAGE
SHRUBS AND VINES		
Myrica asplenifolia	M. pensylvanica	112
Rosa humilis	R. carolina	112
Sassafras variifolium	S. albidum	113
Vaccinium atrococcum	V. corymbosum	113
Vaccinium pennsylvanicum	V. angustifolium	113
Vaccinium virgatum	V. corymbosum	113
Viburnum venosum	V. dentatum var. venosum	113
HERBS		
Ammophila arenaria	A. breviligulata	113
Andropogon scoparius	Schizachyrium scoparium	113
Arctostaphylos Uva-ursi	A. uva-ursi	113
Arenaria peploides	Honckenya peploides	113

Appendix

Corema Conradii	C. conradii	113
Cyperus cylindricus	C. retrotorsus	113
Cyperus Grayii	C. grayii	113
Gerardia flava	Aureolaria virginica	113
Gerardia purpurea	Agalinis purpurea	114
Gerardia setacea	Agalinis setacea	114
Gerardia virginica	Aureoloria flava	114
Lechea villosa	L. mucronata	114
Lespedeza frutescens	L. intermedia	114
Oenothera linearis	O. fructiosa	114
Opuntia vulgaris	O. humifusa	114
Panicum Addisonii	P. commonsianum	114
Panicum Ashei	P. commutatum	114
Panicum Commonsianum	P. commonsianum	114
Panicum Lindheimeri	P. lanuginosum var. lindheimeri	114
Panicum oricola	P. columbianum	114
Panicum tsugetorum	P. columbianum	114
Solidago tenuifolia	Euthamia tenuifolia	114
Spiranthes gracilis	S. lacera	114

Printed in the United States
101699LV00001B/93/A

9 780820 318516